8/04

What
SUCCESSFUL
Teachers Do

What
SUCCESSFUL
Teachers Do

91 Research-Based Classroom Strategies
for New and Veteran Teachers

Neal A. Glasgow ⦿ Cathy D. Hicks

CORWIN PRESS, INC.
A Sage Publications Company
Thousand Oaks, California

For information:

Corwin Press, Inc.
A Sage Publications Company
2455 Teller Road
Thousand Oaks, California 91320
www.corwinpress.com

Sage Publications Ltd.
6 Bonhill Street
London EC2A 4PU
United Kingdom

Sage Publications India Pvt. Ltd.
B-42 Panchsheel Enclave,
Post Box 4109
New Delhi 110 017 India

Printed in the United States of America

Library of Congress Cataloging-in-Publication Data

Glasgow, Neal A.
What successful teachers do : 91 research-based classroom strategies for new and veteran teachers / Neal A. Glasgow, Cathy D. Hicks
    p. cm.
Includes bibliographical references and Index.
ISBN 0-7619-4573-3 (cloth) — ISBN 0-7619-4574-1 (pbk.)
1. Teaching. I. Hicks, Cathy D. II. Title.
LB1025.3 .G516 2003
371.102—dc21

2002011244

This book is printed on acid-free paper.

04   05   06   07   7   6   5   4

Acquisitions Editor:	Faye Zucker
Editorial Assistant:	Julia Parnell
Production Editor:	Olivia Weber
Copyeditor:	Toni Williams
Typesetter:	C&M Digitals (P) Ltd.
Indexer:	Michael Ferreira
Cover Designer:	Michael Dubowe
Production Artist:	Michelle Lee

Contents

Foreword

The interesting thing about successful teachers is that they never stop learning. And this new book about successful teachers by Neal Glasgow and Cathy Hicks, both veteran and master teachers, makes it easy to keep on learning. The format reads like a well thought-out lesson plan: a teaching strategy, the research supporting that strategy, classroom applications, precautions and possible pitfalls, and sources, all designed to provide the teacher with the confidence needed to apply the new teaching strategy in tomorrow's lesson. *What Successful Teachers Do* offers solid research to develop real instructional strategies in brain-based, learning-friendly ways.

After teaching for over 30 years, I am still constantly striving to be a better teacher. And like all busy teachers, I prefer to work smarter, not harder. This books cuts to the chase. There are 12 chapters, each one presenting strategies in categories that are useful both for beginning and for seasoned teachers.

I was hooked the instant I first saw this book. My life has been a search to become a more effective teacher, and I was pulled in by the book title *What Successful Teachers Do*. After 30 years of teaching, however, I have learned to be wary of books that carry messages the likes of "believe and you can achieve." I want proven methods and materials, not feel-good promises. This book delivers with 91 researched-based classroom strategies for teachers in the real world.

The strategies cover the necessarily wide spectrum of important topics for successful teachers: from working with students, colleagues, and parents to managing your classroom, your curriculum, your assessment, your teaching style, and yourself.

Perhaps most important to me is that the authors have written with the underlying belief that students don't care what you teach if you don't teach that you care. They include strategies for dealing with test anxiety and the use of humor to help put students at ease, to gain attention, and to help let the student know that the teacher is indeed an empathetic, caring human being. Successful teachers take time to talk and to listen to their students.

The strategies that encourage peer coaching are invaluable. Even today as I travel the world providing teacher training, I am still amazed that many teachers do not realize the wealth of knowledge and experience in their own buildings. Teachers do not need to suffer in the silence of isolation. They need to talk, share, and grow with their colleagues. One of the most worthwhile strategies is the authors' caveat to surround yourself with mentors who are positive and to avoid the teacher who is negative.

What Successful Teachers Do addresses the timely issues of technology, diversity, and students with special needs, which are of paramount importance for today's educators. The strategies for becoming a professional—such as dressing for respect and results and joining professional growth organizations—are priceless. Many teachers find out about these secrets only after years of experience. The authors also explore an important area that needs more attention for your students and for teachers. It seems as if almost everyone involved with education today is stressing proficiency and standards testing. These are important concerns. But what about reality testing? Do you know about youth culture and how it relates to student health, to school safety, and to learning? Is your classroom youth-culture-friendly? And what about you as a teacher? Teaching is a stressful occupation. Safe and healthy teachers are better teachers who teach more effectively.

The effectiveness of these strategies may vary from teacher to teacher, class to class, school to school, and year to year. Becoming a successful teacher is not a destination, it is a never-ending wonderful journey. And successful teachers continually reflect on their classroom experiences along the way. No matter where you are in your teaching career, this book will take you places you have been, will be, and wish to be. In fact, I have found some strategies that I can't wait to try!

Dr. Stephen Sroka
www.DrStephenSroka.com

Preface

The teaching profession faces a dilemma of monumental proportions, as the need for effective teachers has never been more critical. While it is estimated that over the next 10 years 2 million new teachers will be needed nationwide, research overwhelmingly predicts that 50% of new teachers will not be teaching after three to five years in the profession. An even more alarming statistic states that 17% of new teachers won't even last one year. Of major concern is the realization, supported by research, which shows that teachers don't really learn their craft until they have been teaching at least five to six years. It takes that long for novice teachers to experiment with and adapt the rules and procedures they must employ in their classroom, to develop and refine lesson plans, and to embrace a sense of community and camaraderie with their students and colleagues. Further, we know that professional good teachers continually strive to improve their own professional growth by attending conferences and inservices, collaborating with colleagues, and keeping up with the latest professional journals. Bridging the gap between the crucial need for teachers yet expecting excellence is the challenge that educators, school districts, and institutes of higher education face. We hope this book will serve as a resource for not only beginning teachers but veterans as well, as they develop and polish the skills that will define them as educators throughout their professional career.

This book is not meant to be read as one would read a novel, but rather our objective is to focus on useful and practical educational research that translates into a range of choices and solutions to individual teaching and learning problems typically faced by new teachers. Within these chapters we present a large range of instructional strategies and suggestions based on educational, psychological, and sociological studies. The strategies are based on research done with preservice, student, beginning, or experienced teachers. Strategies within the chapters are structured in a user-friendly format:

- The Strategy: A simple, concise, or crisp statement of an instructional strategy.

- What the Research Says: A brief discussion of the research that led to the strategy. This section should simply give the teacher some confidence in, and a deeper understanding of, the principle(s) being discussed as an instructional strategy.

● Classroom Application: A description of how this teaching strategy can be used in instructional settings.

● Precautions and Possible Pitfalls: Caveats intended to make possible reasonably flawless implementation of the teaching strategy. We try to help teachers avoid common difficulties before they occur.

● Sources: These are provided so that the reader may refer to the original research to discover in more detail the main points of the strategies, research, and classroom applications.

We feel that all teachers may benefit from the practical classroom applications filtered through the research findings. Our hope is that our work can provide advice and support in many of the facets of teaching that can be especially troublesome to all teachers regardless of their experience level. While we know that new and veteran teachers receive advice and support from mentors, veteran colleagues, and induction programs, this book's intent is to bring the reader methodologies based on educational research findings. The strategies provide ideas to strengthen and support classroom theory and practical, reality-based suggestions.

It is our hope that if new teachers accept some of these ideas, maybe they can avoid the "baptism by fire" that many of us experienced when we first started teaching. Veteran teachers can also benefit from knowledge gained from the most recent research. Given the critical need for teachers now and in the future, we, as a profession, cannot afford to have potentially good teachers leaving the profession because they don't feel supported, they're too overwhelmed, or they suffer from burnout.

We feel that as a new teacher reading this book for the first time there may be strategies that presumably don't apply. As in any new endeavor, as a beginning teacher, there may be a tendency of "not knowing what you don't know." We ask that you come back and revisit this book from time to time throughout the year. What may not be applicable the first time you read it may be of help at a later date. Veteran teachers can refresh their teaching toolbox by scanning the range of strategies presented in the book to apply these strategies to their own teaching environment.

Teaching, and education in general, has never been more exciting or more challenging. Expectations for teachers, students, and schools continue to rise. The more resources teachers have at their fingertips to assist students along their educational journey, the better the outcome for all of us. Hopefully, all teachers will find this book useful and practical in defining and enhancing their teaching skills.

Acknowledgments

In a completely rational society, the best of us would be teachers and the rest of us would have to settle for something less, because passing civilization along from one generation to the next ought to be the highest honor and the highest responsibility anyone could have.

Lee Iacocca

We are grateful to the people at Corwin Press, especially Faye Zucker, for their complete collaboration and support. We are also indebted to Alfred Posamentier, Constanze Kaiser, and Hope Hartman for their work on the *Tips for the Mathematics Teacher: Research-Based Strategies to Help Students Learn*, which inspired and provided a model for this book. In addition, we are most appreciative of Adele Lapadula, English Teacher extraordinaire, for her help and suggestions in editing the manuscript. She is the type of teacher and mentor all teachers should aspire to be. We are also thankful to the thousands of students who have been in our classes over the past 25 years and have helped remind us that we teach students, not just subjects. They inspire us to continually want to grow and develop as educators.

Neal Glasgow greatly appreciates Hope Hartman for the opportunities he had to collaborate and learn from her while researching and writing *Tips for the Science Teacher: Research-Based Strategies to Help Students Learn* (for which Neal Glasgow was a coauthor). He is also grateful to the San Dieguito Union High School District and especially San Dieguito Academy High School. Their staff, administration, faculty, and teaching and learning environments constantly provide inspiration and a reason to conduct research and write. The district's new teachers and student teachers never failed to provide the motivation to bring the most valid research-based guidance and information to them. He also acknowledges the University of California, San Diego library staff and resources for providing unlimited and easy access to the world of educational research.

He is also grateful to the "lunch-bunch"—John Ratajkowski, Tim Roberts, and Brian Scott—for almost daily inservices and humorous twists on personal and professional reflection. Finally, he is most indebted to the caring educational researchers and their many students who provided the knowledge to help new teachers not only survive but excel as professionals.

Cathy Hicks is grateful to coauthor Neal Glasgow for his vote of confidence in thinking her experiences in working with new teachers could contribute to this project. While she has had many years of experience working with beginning teachers and has given numerous presentations to them, this has been her first venture into the world of writing. This experience has been both a labor of love and a tremendous learning experience and she thanks Neal for his support and mentorship along the way.

She is also thankful and deeply indebted to the many exemplary teachers and colleagues she has worked with and learned from along her own educational journey. Their influence, dedication, and professionalism have helped remind her of the pivotal role that a teacher's relationship with student, subject, and staff plays in the quest for true excellence in the classroom.

Finally, a thank you to Dr. Rodney Phillips, Cathy's principal and mentor as a first-year teacher. She thanks him for giving a young, idealistic, and enthusiastic teacher the opportunity to experience and take risks, allowing her to learn from her mistakes, while not destroying her spirit. His understanding, advice, and leadership helped a novice teacher begin a love affair with teaching that continues to this day.

Corwin Press acknowledges the important contributions of the following reviewers:

Joyce Harris
Reading/Curriculum Resource Teacher
Title I Resource Team
Covington Independent Schools
Covington, KY

Steve Hutton
Principal
Beechwood Elementary School
Ft. Mitchell, KY

Pat Carlin
French Teacher
Tate's Creek Senior High School
Lexington, KY

Nancy Brennan
Associate
New York State Education Department

Office of Teaching
Albany, NY

Jeanelle Bland
Assistant Professor in Science Education
Eastern Connecticut State University
Willimantic, CT

About the Authors

Neal A. Glasgow has been involved in education on many levels. His experience includes serving as a secondary school science and art teacher both in California and in New York, as a university biotechnology teaching laboratory director and laboratory technician, as an educational consultant, and as a frequent educational speaker on many topics. He is the author of four books on educational topics: *Tips for the Science Teacher: Research-Based Strategies to Help Students Learn* (2001), *New Curriculum for New Times: A Guide to Student-Centered, Problem-Based Learning* (1997), *Doing Science: Innovative Curriculum Beyond the Textbook for the Life Science Classroom* (1997), and *Taking the Classroom Into the Community: A Guide Book* (1996). He is currently teaching biology and art at San Dieguito Academy High School, a California public high school of choice, and continues to conduct research and write on educational topics as well as work on various personal art projects.

Cathy D. Hicks is currently the Beginning Teacher Support and Assessment (BTSA) Coordinator for the San Dieguito Union High School District in Southern California. She oversees a program supporting more than 140 beginning teachers. She serves on the executive board of the California Association of School Health Educators (CASHE) and is on the adjunct faculty of California State University San Marcos, teaching health education for teachers completing their credentials. She has presented at almost a dozen mentor-teacher leader conferences, including "Survival Tips: Helping New Teachers Stay Afloat," "Mentors as Presenters," "Presentation Skills That Impress," and "Hands on Health Education: Lessons from the Trenches." She taught physical education and health at both the middle and high school level for over 25 years. During that time she was involved in the California State Mentor Teacher Program and has been mentoring new teachers in her district for more than 17 years. Her energy, enthusiasm, and passion for teaching and supporting new teachers reinforces the career path she chose in elementary school. She believes the most effective teachers are the ones who never settle for "good enough," but continue to grow, stretch, reflect, create, collaborate, and take risks throughout their teaching careers. She is married and has two grown children.

1

Interacting and Collaborating With Students

 Strategy 1: Look at homework through the eyes of students.

What the Research Says

A new book by Etta Kralovec and John Buell (2000) presents a unique view of the homework concept and questions the value of the practice itself. Few studies have been conducted on the subject and while the book offers perspectives from both sides of the debate, it is clear that the homework concept needs to be examined more closely. For example, Kralovec and Buell cite homework as a great discriminator as children, once leaving school for the day, encounter a range of parental supports, challenging home environments, after-school jobs and sports, and a mix of resources available to some and not to others. Clearly, opportunities are not equal. Tired parents are held captive by the demands of their children's school, unable to develop their own priorities for family life.

Kralovec and Buell also provide examples of communities that have tried to formalize homework policy as the communities tried to balance the demands of homework with extracurricular activities and the need for family time. They also point out the aspects of inequity inherent in the fact many students lack the resources at home to compete on equal footing with those peers who have computers, Internet access, highly educated parents, and unlimited funds and other resources for homework requirements.

They also point out that homework persists despite the lack of any solid evidence that it achieves its much-touted gains. Homework is one of our most entrenched institutional practices, yet one of the least investigated.

The questions their research and discourse explores are, "With single parent households becoming more common or with both parents working, is it reasonable to accept the homework concept, as it is now practiced, as useful and valid considering the tradeoffs families need to make?" "How does homework contribute to family dynamics in negative or positive ways?" "Does it unnecessarily stifle other important opportunities or create an uneven or unequal playing field for some students?"

Classroom Applications

Consider the inequalities that may exist within the range of students in your classes regarding their ability to complete homework assignments. Certain students may be excluded from the opportunities for support and other resources. Consider the following questions:

- What is homework?
- How much homework is too much?
- What are or should be the purposes of homework?
- Can different assignments be given to different students in the same class?
- Do all your students have equal opportunity to successfully complete the homework?
- Who is responsible for homework, the students or the parents?
- Do all your students have the same capacity to self-regulate?
- How are other school activities or family-based responsibilities factored in?
- What is the best and most equitable way to deal with overachievers?
- Is the homework load balanced between teachers?

Precautions and Possible Pitfalls

Traditionally, homework has been seen as a solution rather than the cause of educational problems. It takes a little bit of acclimation time to begin to look at the homework concept with new eyes. However, the value of homework in providing opportunities for students to deepen their general knowledge should not be ignored. This is especially important for students in the United States whose achievement lags behind students from other countries that have longer school days and years. Beware of the politics involved in any discourse regarding the homework concept.

Source

Buell, J., & Kralovec, E. (2000). *The end of homework: How homework disrupts families, overburdens children, and limits learning.* Boston: Beacon.

 Strategy 2: Use the jigsaw technique as an interesting and effective cooperative learning strategy.

What the Research Says

 Contrary to some beliefs about cooperative learning having only social benefits, research shows that the jigsaw method helps students learn and apply academic content as well. An experimental study was conducted with seven classes of students in Grades 7 and 8. The 141 students were separated into four experimental classes and three control classes. The experimental classes were taught with the jigsaw technique, while the three control classes received regular instruction through lectures. The experiment lasted about four weeks, with one double lesson per week. This study examined the social, personal, and academic benefits of jigsaw and traditional instruction. The social and personal benefits observed to result from the jigsaw method are growth of self-control, self-management, ambition, independence, and social interaction. Jigsaw was also found to reduce intimidation in the classroom, which inhibits learning and leads to introverted student behavior. The academic benefits of jigsaw include improved reading abilities, systematic reproduction of knowledge, ability to make conclusions, and summarizing.

When compared with students in traditional classes, students in the jigsaw classrooms demonstrated improved knowledge as well as an ability to apply that knowledge. Students were not afraid to ask questions or to scrutinize presented information when they were able to ask for and receive an explanation from a peer.

Classroom Applications

This example of the jigsaw technique takes place in a physics class and is meant to explore theory and application in an authentic context. The jigsaw technique operates in six steps:

1. Separate a new part of the curriculum into five major sections.

2. Split a class of 25 students into five groups of five students each. These groups are the *base groups*. (The groups should be heterogeneous in terms of gender, cultural background, and achievement levels).

3. Every member of the base group selects or is assigned one of the major sections. For example, one member might focus on the section on the physics of light, another might focus on the section on energy conversion for photosynthesis, while another focuses on the section on vision, neurons, and sight, and so forth. If the number of group members exceeds the number of sections, two students can focus on the same section.

4. The base groups temporarily divide up so each student can join a new group in order to become an "expert" in his or her topic. All the students focusing on the physics of light will be in one group, all the students focusing on energy conversion in photosynthesis will be in another group, and so on. These students work together in temporary groups called *expert groups*. There they learn about their topic and discuss how to teach it to students in their base groups.

5. Students return to their base groups and serve as the expert for their topics. Everyone then takes a turn teaching what he or she learned about his or her topic to members of the base group.

A written test is given to the entire class. In steps 4 and 5 students have an opportunity to discuss and exchange knowledge. Step 6 gives the teacher an opportunity to check the quality of students' work and to see what and how much they learned from each other. One of the advantages of this method of cooperative learning is that in jigsaw there is always active learning going on and students do not become bored while passively listening to reports from other groups, as sometimes happens with the Johnson and Johnson learning together method.

Precautions and Possible Pitfalls

Cooperative learning simply does not work in all classes. Each class comes with its individual social mix that can make or break your cooperative learning attempts. It is also suggested that you wait until you have your class discipline and management plans in place and *working* before attempting cooperative learning strategies.

While students teach members of their base groups in step 5, teachers are frequently tempted to join in the discussions and advise students regarding the best way to teach the subject to their base group. This type of teacher intervention prevents the social and intellectual benefits of jigsaw. Although a teacher has to monitor group work in order to intervene when there are substantial mistakes in understanding the academic content, the teacher should not interfere with how students decide to teach this content to their peers.

Sources

Aronson, E., Blaney, N., Stephan, C., Sikes, J., & Snapp, M. (1978). *The jigsaw classroom*. Beverly Hills, CA: Sage.

Eppler, R., & Huber, G. L. (1990). Wissenswert im Team: Empirische Untersuchung von Effekten des Gruppen-Puzzles [Acquisition of knowledge in teams: An empirical study of effects of the jigsaw techniques]. *Psychologie in Erziehung und Unterricht, 37*, 172-178.

Johnson, D., & Johnson, R. (1975). *Learning together and alone: Cooperation, competition, and individualization*. Englewood Cliffs, NJ: Prentice Hall.

Strategy 3: Manage student-controlled peer interaction within a cooperative framework. Be aware of how student-learning opportunities are affected by student-controlled peer interaction within collaborative work in socially and academically integrated classes.

What the Research Says

Schools are expected to give students insight into content knowledge, learning techniques, reasoning, and logic, while learning a variety of specific processes and applications. In addition, we expect class activity to be conducted in a manner that gives all students equal opportunities for learning and personal development. The focus of this study centered on the activity between students and their peers and students and the teacher, both within the arena of science teaching and learning.

The study centered on the observation of two eighth-grade girls within a science class, from very different social and academic backgrounds. The researchers found the dynamics of student interactions in the specific lessons analyzed did not give all students the same opportunity for learning, and the two girls seemed to be at two different ends of the learning scale. Their conclusions found a very clear "unofficial" classroom arena of discourse and dialogue. This discourse was very much controlled by the students and it seemed to result in a student-controlled differentiation in the integrated classroom. In very subtle ways teachers and students construct opportunities and limitations for each other through their actions.

Looking at student interactions beyond the traditional variables of gender, class, or ethnicity can deepen analysis of the learning environment during science lessons. The study points out that discovery learning and group work may not lead to a discovery of science concepts. Rather it leads to a student's social creativity and to opportunities for identity construction within groups. These constructs can detract rather than enhance a student's opportunity to learn. In an integrated setting, strategies that are supposed to equalize differences between students can create inequities. A second study identified the components of a successful approach and framework for the inclusion of social planning into academic experiences.

Classroom Applications

One cannot analyze a lesson as if it was one lesson for a number of similar students. Rather one has to look at the subtexts in the classroom—at the varying aspects of life in the social beehive of a school class. Most studies see the classroom dominated by teacher-dominated discourse. The classroom also provides an arena for a number of less formal student-dominated discourses. Without more in-depth consideration, the lessons may not provide the same opportunities for all the students.

To begin, be sure to consciously try to deal with the nonintegrative consequences of free choice of seating by assigning students to desk partners that are at different levels of ability and from different backgrounds. Be aware of and discuss, with students, the potential imbalances in opportunities for classroom participation that could also lessen the quality in which students experience instruction. Discuss the ways the domination of the social constructs by certain students limit other students' opportunities for learning and participation.

In spite of the potential problems group dynamics present, unofficial dialogue, small-group work, and peer learning offer opportunities for learning that whole-class teaching cannot. Interactive patterns of small-group work enable contributions from a larger number of students.

The carefully crafted situated nature of learning in which the social aspects of the classroom and beyond are taken into consideration play an essential role in student learning. Many recent studies are framed by the notion that students and teachers create discourse communities in which learning social aspects regarding the construction of content knowledge needs to be a significant part of curricular planning. Carefully orchestrating interdependency in small-group work, public sharing, collaboration with experts, and a redefinition of responsibility in learning and teaching transform students into active learners.

However, the organization of such relationships needs to be routinely considered along with content and assessment. Research suggests that paying attention to the following themes in collaborative curriculum development can serve as a framework.

- Tasks related to real-world questions generate more instructional support than topic-bound tasks—embed your content coverage in motivating questions.
- Collaborative interactions in groups increases when tasks are student initiated.
- Providing instructional support for students contributes to group decision making.
- Group productivity increases when students gain ownership.
- Student dialogue centers on the procedural aspects of the activity when completing teacher-designed activities.
- When student dialogue centers on their own experiences students are more cognitively engaged.
- Interactions with outside resource people increase student investment in the project.

Precautions and Possible Pitfalls

 New teachers should be aware how easy it is to fall into a comfortable pattern of classroom organization. Discipline management often takes precedence over teaching and learning management. Classroom social and academic organizations that yield class control and discipline may not always provide the less restrictive and most beneficial learning environment for the greatest number of students. You may have to accept a few less-mature students falling through the cracks so that others can benefit from different learning and teaching arrangements.

Reorganizing academic social arrangements is not always popular with students and may cause friction. Often informal social and peer group arrangements affect learning more than a teacher's more formal strategies. Keep the bigger picture in mind and maximize the benefits of effective strategies for the greatest number of students.

Sources

Crawford, B. A., Krajcik, J. S., & Marx, R. W. (1999). Elements of a community of learners in a middle school science classroom. *Science Education, 83*(6), 701-723.

Sahlstrom, F., & Lindblad, S. (1998). Subtexts in the science classroom—and exploration of the social construction of science lessons and school careers. *Learning and Instruction, 8*(3), 195-214.

 Strategy 4: Teach students to use self-questioning and think-aloud techniques. This will help them become more aware of and more able to control their reasoning and problem solving.

What the Research Says

Educators (e.g., Baird & White, 1984; Narode, Heiman, Lochhead, & Slomianko, 1987) suggest self-questioning and think-aloud processes are effective strategies to promote problem solving. Baird and White conducted a study designed to improve metacognition in ninth-grade students learning science and 11th graders learning biology. They identified the following seven learner objectives:

1. Increased knowledge of metacognition

2. Enhanced awareness of their learning styles

3. Greater awareness of the purposes and natures of tasks

4. More control over learning through better decision making

5. More positive attitudes toward learning

6. Higher standards for understanding and performance set by the students themselves and more precise self-evaluation of their achievements

7. Greater effectiveness as independent learners, planning thoughtfully, diagnosing learning difficulties and overcoming them, and using time more productively

Instructional materials included a question-asking checklist, evaluation of learning behaviors and outcomes, a notebook, and a techniques workbook where students tried out concept mapping. This extensive study went through four phases and involved 15 methods of collecting data, including video and audiotapes, classroom observations, questionnaires, and tests. The results showed increased student control over learning and understanding content.

Classroom Applications

How do professionals in any career think and reason, conduct their work, and keep learning and being creative? Are the career skills required similar? How do problem solvers and creative people in any discipline create an intellectually rich and fertile mental environment? Some thinking and reasoning strategies are more conducive to making discoveries and bringing clarity of understanding.

Self-questioning and think-aloud techniques are routinely practiced within the context of research laboratory and office team meetings everywhere. Original and creative processing has gone from an individual process to more of a group enterprise as reasoning and knowledge are

Table 1.1   Universal Self-Questions

Planning	Monitoring	Evaluating
1. How can I design situations to test my ideas?	1. Does the initial plan meet my needs or does it need adjusting?	1. How effective was my self-reflection of my work?
2. What are all of the critical elements that need to be considered?	2. Should I try a different approach?	2. To what degree were my conclusions or final results justified by research materials or gathered information?
3. What elements of learning or knowledge bases need to be addressed or acquired?	3. Am I processing all my work and effort accurately?	3. What useful feedback did I get from others?
4. How can I show that learning and understanding have taken place?	4. Am I covering, observing, and recording everything I'm supposed to?	4. How could I improve as a consumer of information?

distributed among many stakeholders within a specific laboratory, office, company, or agency. The more diverse the group, the more beneficial shared reasoning and knowledge become. The following are a few basic suggestions to focus on while using these types of instructional strategies.

• Use self-questioning and think-aloud techniques within cooperative groups to distribute reasoning and knowledge within the group. This is especially important within the context of inquiry-based learning activities.

• Have students follow up on surprising results or ideas. Pay attention to unexpected findings in the control conditions because these results can lead to other fruitful learning and teaching pathways.

• Have students engage in analytical reasoning both in formulating and asking good questions, hypothesizing, and solving research or investigative problems and in synthesizing new ideas along the way. Think out loud using distant analogies as an explanatory device. Have students refer back to other experiences where similar thinking frameworks were used. Make frequent use of analogies as explanations (a common way professionals converse).

• During self-questioning and thinking out loud activities, make sure the students' current goals are not blocking them from considering alternative theories or ways of looking at content and other learning activities.

Table 1.1 presents some examples of more universal self-questions.

Precautions and Possible Pitfalls

 Given classroom peer pressures, students critiquing each other's questions may be a challenge for the teacher. Avoid embarrassing students who ask ineffective questions by not calling attention to them in a whole-class setting.

Group work presents many pitfalls. Not all students will feel comfortable using these techniques or will buy into your strategies. You will have to decide how involved you want your students to become in this type of instructional strategy. If the process becomes too contrived, it loses its effectiveness. Closely monitor your groups. The more routine this type of discourse becomes and the more practiced the students, the more their comfort level will rise. To begin, consider having each group engage in these strategies while the others watch as a way to maintain control, guide, and reinforce positive behaviors.

Teachers who attempt this suggestion for implementation must be aware that this is meant to be an enhancement for the instructional program and not a deterrent. If one technique doesn't seem to work with a particular class, it ought to be replaced with a more effective approach.

Sources

Baird, J., & White, R. (1984). *Improving learning through enhanced metacognition: A classroom study*. Paper presented at the annual meeting of the American Educational Research Association, New Orleans, LA.

Brown, G. A., & Edmondson, R. (1984). Asking questions. In E. C. Wragg (Ed.), *Classroom teaching skills*. New York: Nichols.

Dunbar, K. (2000). How scientists think in the real world. *Journal of Applied Developmental Psychology, 21*(1), 49-58.

Narode, R., Heiman, M., Lochhead, J., & Slomianko, J. (1987). *Teaching thinking skills: Science*. Washington, DC: National Educational Association.

 Strategy 5: Help students learn to reflect on their own academic successes and failures. They can learn to accurately create, monitor, analyze, and control their own explanations for their academic successes and failures.

What the Research Says

Students often get into ruts in school, falsely thinking that because they didn't do well in a class in the past, they won't now or in the future. However, extensive research shows that students can learn to control their own academic destinies. One body of research focuses on students' attributions for success and failure. This research shows there are four common reasons people give for their successes and failures: ability, effort, task difficulty, and luck. Attributions can be divided into two dimensions: stable-unstable and internal-external. *Stable-unstable* refers to how consistent the attributions are over time. That is, the extent to which a person uses the same types of reasons to explain his or her success or failure over and over again (stable) or whether the person gives one kind of reason on one occasion and another type of reason another time (unstable). For example, Lillian says solving mass problems in physics is always too difficult for her (stable) but that in chemistry some balancing equation problems are easy for her and some are too difficult (unstable). Stable arguments are often harder to address. They tend to be avoidance arguments; that is, the student consistently uses the same argument to avoid work he or she feels threatened by. Older students tend to form defensive "stable" arguments to avoid potential "failure" situations.

Internal-external refers to a situation where a person assigns responsibility for his or her successes and failures—inside or outside the self. For example, Lillian says she didn't do well on her test about the Holocaust because she didn't study enough (internal). Lillian says she didn't do well on her first science test because her family interfered with her study time (external). She says she got a good grade on her second science test because she was lucky (external).

Students' explanations of their successes and failures have important consequences for future performance on academic tasks. Research shows there are four common ways students explain their successes and failures: effort ("I could do it if I really tried"), ability ("I'm just not a good writer"), luck ("I guessed right"), and task difficulty ("The test was too hard") (Alderman, 1990, p. 37). Attributions are related to the following:

- Expectations about one's likelihood of success
- Judgments about one's ability
- Emotional reactions of pride, hopelessness, and helplessness
- Willingness to work hard and self-regulate one's efforts

Classroom Applications

Help students rid themselves of their misconceptions about learning. Students who see a relationship between their effort and their success are more likely to use learning strategies such as organizing, planning, goal setting, self-checking, and self-instruction. Alderman's links to success model is designed to help at risk students develop attributions that will motivate them to succeed. Her four links to success are as follows:

1.   *Proximal goals*, which are short term rather than long term, specific rather than general, and hard (but reachable) rather than easy; e.g., "This week I'll manage my time so that I have three extra hours to study." Teach students to anticipate and overcome obstacles, monitor progress while goals are being pursued, and evaluate whether they achieved their goals at the end of the specified time. "I'll know whether I accomplished this goal by writing down how much time I study and comparing that to how much I studied last week." Obstacles to achieving this goal may be addressed by a statement such as, "I will overcome these obstacles by. . . ." When they don't achieve their goals, teach students to determine why and what they could do differently next time.

2.   *Learning strategies*, which students are taught so they can apply effective strategies, such as summarizing and clarifying, that emphasize meaningful learning and can be used across subjects and situations, instead of ineffective approaches, such as repeating, which tends to emphasize rote memorization.

3.   *Success experiences*, where students evaluate their success in achieving the proximal goals and where learning ("How much progress did I make?") rather than performance ("What grade did I get?") is the goal.

4.   *Attributions for success*, where students are encouraged to explain their successes in terms of their personal efforts or abilities. The teacher's role here is to give students feedback on why they succeeded or failed and help students give the appropriate explanation. Was an answer incorrect, incomplete, or was there a careless mistake? Make sure students understand why an answer is incorrect. Ask questions such as, "What did you do when you tried to answer that question or solve that problem?"

Precautions and Possible Pitfalls

Feelings of helplessness are created over a period of time through the belief that failure is due to lack of ability, so it is important for students to learn that their ability can improve if they use proper strategies and make appropriate efforts. Students want to resist being put in positions of failure and are often more motivated by fear of failure than by your "new" strategies for success. Occasionally, and usually with older students, you will find your efforts simply won't work. Don't give up on all students because a few have given up on themselves. Be careful not to alienate those few because they aren't buying into your best efforts.

Source

Alderman, M. K. (1990, September). Motivation for at-risk students. *Educational Leadership*, 27-30.

Strategy 6: Match student study skills to the learning environment.

What the Research Says

The importance of an individual-based analysis of the study orientations of your students is examined in this research. Sixty-seven high achievers completed a questionnaire that focused on their study practices and conceptions of knowledge. Individual ways students interact with their learning environment are surveyed.

The results show a connection between a student's study orchestration and study success. There may be a conflict between the requirements of the learning environment and the student's individual study practices. In addition, the learning environment may yield misleading clues about how to study effectively. It was concluded that poor study practices might develop because of a mismatch between the demands of the learning environment and the student's personal goals.

The studies suggest that students' conceptions of learning, approaches to learning, and levels of processing learning activities can be divided into two categories: surface-level reproduction (or memorizing) and deep-level transformation (or construction) of knowledge. The latter is associated with more meaningful learning.

In a related dimension, how students self-regulated their learning environment was considered. Students may differ in terms of their ability to express self-regulation and depend on external regulation or they may lack regulatory skills all together. Self-regulation is most often related to the deep approach to learning whereas external regulation is more likely associated with the surface approach.

Successful students were able to use flexible strategies according to the course demands and use the strategies that are the most appropriate to a specific learning environment. Therefore, the development of the students' metacognitive skills is a very important component in developing study practices or replacing less effective learning habits with more effective ones.

Classroom Applications

Occasionally students will have difficulty studying your content area's topics, yet do very well in other disciplines. The skills that work in one discipline don't always transfer to others. Students often gauge their overall success, failure, and level of frustration by how much effort they feel they brought to a learning activity. When you hear an "effort" argument from a student, it often means that the student's effort was misguided or ineffective, which can lead a student to opt out of a learning environment. The effort argument often results from conflicts between the class environment and the students' study skills and habits. The same effort in one class may not yield the same level of success as in others. How can you help these students?

The study cited points to a need to quantitatively analyze students' approaches to studying and learning orientations to get an overview of the students' study orientations. Just asking students to describe their subjective definitions of learning can give a teacher great insight. This leads students into self-reflection about their own studying and learning styles. Self-reflection is done as a self-assessment inventory for the student's use as well. It provides the students with an opportunity to talk about their results with teachers. Once the results are known it is also possible to reorganize the learning environment.

Where do you find the resources to create such an inventory? Type the phrase "learning styles" into an Internet search engine. You will find many sites that contain information on how to assess learning styles and effective personal study strategies. Also, there have been many books and papers written that provide tools to inventory such information.

The lack of effective study strategies interferes with your students' ability to be successful in your class. Students with disintegrated perceptions of their learning environment often lack a commitment to the academic environment and to their purposes of studying. Taking time out of more specific content goals and objectives to address these issues may serve the students' needs in a richer and more meaningful way.

Numerous print and online resources on programs and materials are available to help students develop study skills specifically oriented toward your discipline. An early program with a history of success with high school students in some disciplines is "Stress on Analytical Reasoning" (SOAR). Another successful program for helping students make the transition from high school to college by developing their ability to think abstractly instead of concretely is Development of Reasoning in Science (DORIS). One especially useful print resource for the sciences is *Teaching Thinking Skills: Science* (Narode, Heiman, Lochhead, & Slomianko, 1987).

Precautions and Possible Pitfalls

Teachers need to cultivate the ability to determine what really motivates specific students to replace or reorganize their study efforts. Teaching and acquiring effective study habits should become an ongoing part of a hidden curriculum. Don't be disappointed if your efforts to teach study skills do not produce the desired or expected results. Different student demographics and levels of buy-in require different levels of guided practice, attention, and external versus internal reward structures.

Teachers sometimes have problems replacing direct content or discipline work with curriculum that doesn't directly relate to the subject area. With all the testing done today, teachers find it hard to give up class time to teach study skills. Try to integrate study techniques directly into content work. Students need to know that reading a novel is different than reading a science or math book. Teach reading skills that relate to your discipline. In the end students will become more successful as overall learners when you take the time to teach them how to more effectively learn to learn!

Sources

Lindblom-Ylanne, S., & Lonka, K. (1999). Individual ways of interacting with the learning environment: Are they related to study success? *Learning and Instruction, 9,* 1-18.

Narode, R., Heiman, M., Lochhead, J., & Slomianko, J. (1987). *Teaching thinking skills: Science.* Washington, DC: National Education Association.

Nickerson, R., Perkins, D., & Smith, E. (1985). *The teaching of thinking.* Hillsdale, NJ: Erlbaum.

 Strategy 7: Teach students how to work cooperatively. Structure classroom activities so that students learn that teamwork is common in professional endeavors.

What the Research Says

 When students cooperate with other students, they often get more out of learning than they do when working on their own or even when working with the teacher. When students are isolated from each other and consequently compete with each other, they are less involved in learning, their learning is not as deep, and they have fewer opportunities to improve their thinking. Students who work cooperatively absorb more and higher-level subject-area knowledge, knowledge which they retain and apply when working on difficult tasks more effectively than students who work individually. Additionally, cooperative learning situations motivate students to learn because learning becomes fun and meaningful; it boosts students' self-esteem as they explain content to others and it improves interpersonal relationships between culturally diverse students. Finally, working cooperatively develops students' higher-level thinking skills, such as metacognition, as students compare their own knowledge and strategies with that of others. Professionals seldom work in isolation; they usually require input and feedback from their peers to extend and refine their own thinking. Often scientific enterprise is conducted through teams, with individuals cooperating with each other on a project, and through teams cooperating with other teams.

Classroom Applications

 One example of an activity where cooperative learning may be beneficial is to have students investigate or solve a problem such as the following.

This earth science activity is an application of plate tectonics basics with a bit of oceanography and biology thrown in. To implement this procedure, set up groups of between two and four students. Students are given latitude and longitude coordinates in the Mid-Atlantic Ocean. Their job is to design and hypothesize their vision of an island based on local geology if it formed at the location. The teacher gives the island an age of 60,000 years and asks the students to describe what the island's life might look like, as well as how life would have appeared.

The teacher continues to introduce and build the project, analyzing ocean currents and weather patterns. Each student acquires a piece of the island's natural history to study, learn, and describe. The teacher helps the students create a rubric (which will eventually become a table of contents) to help them structure their project. Four students eventually divide up the tasks and keep the communication going to keep the project components cohesive.

The teacher has just modeled the thinking in which he or she wants the students to engage. Each student has an important piece of the project to complete. The project is very open-ended and these amateur naturalists can delve as deep as they like into the content's complexity. Climate and weather information may be found on the Internet. Students locate adjacent islands as references. They dive back into the biology lessons on Darwin and the Galapagos Islands. The central thread is their island, but the range of scientific concepts is huge. In the end, outcomes can include a paper or presentation. It is hard for any group member to fall through the cracks. Each partner has too big a stake. This project, with its range of problems, is rich in opportunities for group work.

An excellent resource for planning cooperative learning activities in science for both elementary and middle school classrooms is Hassard's (1990) *Science Experiences: Cooperative Learning and the Teaching of Science*.

While the example here deals with a science activity, many other disciplines provide themes and concepts to construct units around team-building pedagogy. The key is to develop different learning pathways or aspects within the same concept. Large themes or concepts can be broken down into smaller units that overlap and complement one another. Each student can assume responsibility for an individual piece of the concept or theme.

Students can then work individually or in small groups within the same concept or theme, yet on related but slightly different overlapping pathways. In this way, overlapping resources can help students build a deeper and more multifaceted view of the curricular target, yet each student takes responsibility for an individual piece of the theme or concept.

Precautions and Possible Pitfalls

Not all group work is cooperative learning. Students must work together, help each other, and learn from each other—not just find factual answers together—in order for the process to really be cooperative learning. Watch that one person doesn't dominate the group, which often tends to occur. Assigning group roles is one way of either preventing this from occurring or handling it when it does occur. Effective group work takes effort. Teachers need to constantly monitor groups as they are solving problems to make sure they stay on task and are working in productive ways. While some teachers suggest using cooperative learning across the board, most research indicates that careful selection of problems for use in cooperative learning groups is important. Research on the effectiveness of cooperative learning in classrooms indicates it works more suitably with some content problems and skills than others. Easy problems are unlikely to work effectively in cooperative learning groups because there is less need to collaborate and help each other.

Don't let students form their own groups; working with friends can inhibit learning. Carefully set up the groups in advance to maximize diversity, using as many variables as possible including gender, cultural and linguistic background, achievement, personality, and social characteristics. Johnson and Johnson (1975) emphasize the importance of training students in cooperative skills such as giving feedback, asking questions, and listening before cooperative learning begins. This practice will ensure that the groups function effectively. They also recommend *group processing* at the end of a cooperative learning activity so students can evaluate their individual and group performance (e.g., Did anyone dominate the discussion? How well did the group stay on task?) and plan for future improvements. Teachers should try building individual assessment responsibilities into activities, not just group grades.

Sources

Hassard, J. (1990). *Science experiences: Cooperative learning and the teaching of science.* Menlo Park, CA: Addison-Wesley.

Johnson, D., & Johnson, R. (1975). *Learning together and alone: Cooperation, competition, and individualization.* Englewood Cliffs, NJ: Prentice Hall.

Slavin, R. (1990). *Cooperative learning: Theory, research and practice.* Englewood Cliffs, NJ: Prentice Hall.

Strategy 8: Help students overcome test anxiety. Be aware of students' different levels of test anxiety as they relate to different subject areas and use a variety of techniques to help them overcome their test anxiety.

What the Research Says

Students have different degrees of test anxiety for different subject areas. One study (Everson, Tobias, Hartman, & Gourgey, 1993) compared 196 first-year college students' self-reports of test anxiety in mathematics, physical sciences, English, and social studies. Students were administered the Worry-Emotionality Scale in which they rated their anxiety about tests in one of these four subjects. The directions asked them to imagine they were taking a test in mathematics, for example, and to rate their feelings on a five-point scale ranging from "I would not feel that way at all" (1) to "I would feel that way very strongly" (5). Questions included, "I would feel my heart beating fast" and "I would feel that I should have studied more for that test." In rank order from most test anxiety to least test anxiety, the subjects were physical sciences, mathematics, English, and social studies. For elementary and secondary school students, test anxiety is often developed from a combination of factors. These factors include parents' early reactions to their children's poor test performance, students' comparisons of their performance with other students or siblings as well as their own prior test performance, and increasingly strict evaluation practices as students progressed through school. For low-achieving students, failure experiences tend to increase test anxiety. For high-achieving students, unrealistically high self-, parental, and peer expectations tend to increase test anxiety. Some classroom practices affect test anxiety. Presenting material in an organized way and making sure it isn't too hard tends to improve the performance of test-anxious students.

Classroom Applications

Test anxiety interferes with test performance. Students waste mental energy on anxiety that they could be using to answer the test questions. There are many strategies teachers can suggest and demonstrate to students to help them relax. First find out what strategies they already use. Share with them techniques you use to relax. Try to reduce the pressure students feel from being assessed and evaluated by tests. Using other assessment strategies and more traditional tests can help reduce the pressure of being evaluated by tests and the corresponding test anxiety. Help students learn to differentiate between constructive and destructive instances of anxiety. In constructive or facilitative anxiety, students see tests as challenging experiences. In destructive or debilitative anxiety, students see tests as negative self-evaluation experiences. Teach students to become aware of and control their anxiety before, during, and after testing. For example, ask them "What thoughts go through your mind before taking a test?" "What kinds of thoughts do you have while you are taking a test?" Help students improve their study strategies and test-taking skills. Demonstrate and encourage use of the assorted relaxation techniques described below.

Deep Breathing

With erect posture, breathe in deeply through the nose and hold your breath for a count of 8-10. Then, slowly exhale through the mouth, counting 8-10. Repeat this procedure several times until relaxation occurs.

Muscle Relaxation

Tension-Relaxation

Tighten and then relax a muscle or set of muscles that normally store considerable tension, such as your shoulders. Hold the muscles in a tensed state for a few seconds and then let go. Repeat this sequence with the same muscles a few times and then move on to other muscles.

Self-Hypnosis

Sit straight in a chair with arms and legs uncrossed, feet flat on the floor, and palms on top of your thighs. Progressively relax your body, from toes to head, systematically focusing on one part at a time. Concentrate on tuning into your bodily sensations, allowing your muscles to relax, becoming more aware of what it feels like when your muscles are relaxed. Talk to yourself (aloud or silently) telling yourself to loosen up and lessen the tightness. When the body is relaxed, it is more receptive to positive self-talk. Build up your self-confidence at this point. For example, "I know I can do well on this test!"

Creative Visualization

Guide students in engaging in success-imagery minutes, days, and weeks before testing.

Olympic Success

Tell them to try what the Olympic athletes do to develop confidence in their performance. Picture yourself in a tense situation, such as taking a test, and visualize yourself looking over the test, seeing the questions, and feeling secure about the answers. Imagine yourself answering the questions without too much difficulty. Complete the picture by imagining yourself turning in the paper and leaving the room assured that you did your best.

Relaxing Place

Where do your students feel most at peace? One spot could be at the ocean. Have students identify a place and use all their senses to imagine themselves there and how they feel when they are there. Guide them in an activity: *Watch* the waves with their whitecaps rolling up the shoreline onto the beach. *Listen* to the waves and the seagulls. *Smell* the salty air and *feel* your fingers and toes in the warm, soft, and grainy sand.

Precautions and Possible Pitfalls

Whatever a teacher decides to do in this regard must be done with a modicum of reserve, assessing the audience members and their reaction. Not all suggestions work with all students. Make sure to encourage students not to give up if the first relaxation technique doesn't work. Often these techniques need to be practiced to be successful, and often students must experiment with a variety of techniques to determine which ones work best for them. Ask your students questions to see whether gender or cultural differences might affect the use of these suggestions and to elicit ideas you might not have previously considered.

Sources

Everson, H. T., Tobias, S., Hartman, H., & Gourgey, A. (1993). Test anxiety and the curriculum: The subject matters. *Anxiety, Stress and Coping, 6,* 1-8.

Hartman, H. (1997). *Human learning and instruction.* New York: City University of New York.

Strategy 9: Lighten your load by training students to be tutors. Student tutors can specialize in helping students (especially the educationally challenged) through difficult parts of classroom activities.

What the Research Says

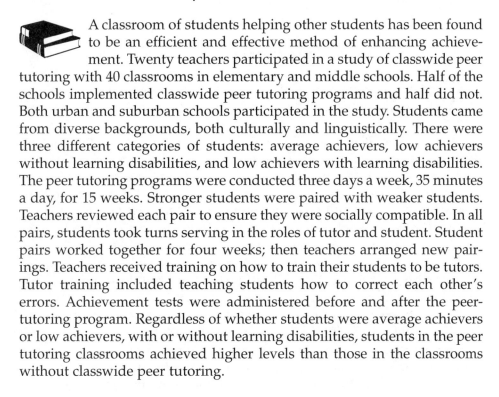 A classroom of students helping other students has been found to be an efficient and effective method of enhancing achievement. Twenty teachers participated in a study of classwide peer tutoring with 40 classrooms in elementary and middle schools. Half of the schools implemented classwide peer tutoring programs and half did not. Both urban and suburban schools participated in the study. Students came from diverse backgrounds, both culturally and linguistically. There were three different categories of students: average achievers, low achievers without learning disabilities, and low achievers with learning disabilities. The peer tutoring programs were conducted three days a week, 35 minutes a day, for 15 weeks. Stronger students were paired with weaker students. Teachers reviewed each pair to ensure they were socially compatible. In all pairs, students took turns serving in the roles of tutor and student. Student pairs worked together for four weeks; then teachers arranged new pairings. Teachers received training on how to train their students to be tutors. Tutor training included teaching students how to correct each other's errors. Achievement tests were administered before and after the peer-tutoring program. Regardless of whether students were average achievers or low achievers, with or without learning disabilities, students in the peer tutoring classrooms achieved higher levels than those in the classrooms without classwide peer tutoring.

Classroom Applications

There are many areas in all content classes that lend themselves to a peer-tutoring program. When there is a skill to be learned and all one needs is experience with success (i.e., drill with immediate feedback), then peer tutoring could provide an efficient way to monitor and support a student trying to master the skill. Say a student has difficulty identifying an unknown chemical, an anion, or a cation. Individual students within groups can specialize as peer tutors in specific chemical tests or flame tests, or a general peer tutor (under the guidance of a teacher) can be quite beneficial. There are many tests at which peer tutors can become expert and then share their expertise with individual students. A student who has difficulty doing these tests could find that a peer tutor is a genuine asset.

Foreign-language classes are a natural for tutoring. Advanced students can routinely help less-skilled language students. Rather than waiting for an opportunity to talk with the teacher, a student has access to the peer tutor, saving everyone time. Additionally, in explaining the methodology to the student, the tutor is also provided with an opportunity to strengthen his or her own understanding of the concept of test reactions or a specific element of language (a higher-order thinking skill). Thus, there is often a mutual benefit to a peer-tutoring program.

Precautions and Possible Pitfalls

Not every student makes a good tutor. Some are not mature enough to manage the responsibility. A tutor-training program offered by the teacher can precede peer tutoring. Some kids are natural tutors while some must be given some instruction on how to conduct the specific concepts or sessions, what sort of difficulties to look for on the part of the tutee, and what points to stress in the sessions (based on the teacher's assessment of the class). Any individual difficulties on the part of the tutees should be mentioned to the tutor prior to the sessions. Tutors should be taught to guide student learning and *not* merely solve problems for students. Students with severe learning disabilities may not be receptive to tutoring or benefit from classwide peer tutoring, unless the tutors first receive individualized instruction from learning disability specialists.

Finally, there may be classes into which a tutoring system simply doesn't fit. Classes with discipline problems or classes with homogeneous learners may not provide the best setting to begin a tutoring program. In some cases managing tutors in tough classes can be more trouble than it is worth. The teacher should carefully consider the class before committing to this method.

Source

Fuchs, D., Fuchs, L., Mathes, P. G., & Simmons, D. (1997). Peer-assisted learning strategies: Making classrooms more responsive to diversity. *American Educational Research Journal, 34*(1), 174-206.

Strategy 10: Be sensitive to possible gender and ethnic differences.

What the Research Says

Historically, girls and certain ethnic minority groups have underachieved in schools. This is especially true in science and math classes. Research suggests that girls and boys may have different science preferences and self-perceptions depending upon the specific area of science. Fourth-grade girls were found to prefer biological science while boys preferred physical sciences

(Kahle & Damnjanovic, 1994, 1997). This may impose obstacles to success for students inside and outside the classroom. Stereotypes often convey incorrect explanatory information about specific groups, such as blacks are lazy, girls are bad at science and math, and so forth, that may be used as negative attributions for performance by adults and the children themselves.

One study identified three underlying attributional structures of all stereotypes:

1.   Stereotypes that when used become internal controllable attributions and explanations for controllable behaviors or states of affairs and imply internal, stable, controllable causes. Examples: Whites are bigoted, certain girls are promiscuous, Mexicans are lazy, and so on.

2.   Stereotypes that suggest a trait, attribute, or behavior that is beyond the person's control. Examples: Jocks are dumb, old people are senile, women are weak, Irish are lucky, and so on.

3.   Stereotypes that imply external causes that lie outside the individual being stereotyped and remove responsibility and place it on factors outside the students' control. Examples: Believing some groups are underprivileged by a racist society or believing African Americans and Latinos (as a group) are not as successful as whites because they are lazy or inept.

It was found that each one of these attributional signatures has specific effects on judgments of responsibility. Recognizing that stereotypes are vehicles for attribution judgments, educators can better prepare themselves to deal with the effects that stereotypes may have on students and their perceptions. Then they are better able to counteract or diminish them.

Classroom Applications

Classrooms are increasingly characterized by ethnic diversity, and this trend will continue to become even stronger. Teachers often have unconscious stereotypes of students based on their ethnicity and gender. It is very important for teachers to treat each student as an individual and to tune into and understand each student's thoughts and feelings about learning each discipline.

Precautions and Possible Pitfalls

Beware of stereotyping students based on gender or ethnicity! Although there are general trends for girls versus boys (e.g., preferring biology to physics) and for students from different ethnic groups, teachers should not assume their students to have any predisposed characteristics. Teachers can subtly communicate a self-fulfilling bias or expectation for their students. Keep your expectations high for all students.

Sources

Kahle, J. B., & Damnjanovic, A. (1994). The effects of inquiry activities on elementary students' enjoyment, ease and confidence in doing science: An analysis by sex and race. *Journal of Women and Minorities in Science and Engineering, 1,* 17-28.

Kahle, J. B., & Damnjanovic, A. (1997). How research helps address gender equity. *Research Matters to the Science Teacher, 9703,* 1-5.

Reyna, C. (2000). Lazy, dumb, or industrious: When stereotypes convey attributions information in the classroom. *Educational Psychology Review, 12*(1).

Strategy 11: Use different motivational strategies for girls and boys.

What the Research Says

 When it comes to motivation, girls tend to be generalists while boys tend to be specialists. Interest, rather than intellect, often lies at the heart of the differences between boys and girls in specific discipline areas. Girls tend to be interested in a wide range of subjects, while boys tend to concentrate their interests more narrowly.

A study was conducted with 457 students; 338 students attended special mathematics and science-oriented schools while 119 students attended regular schools but had excellent grades in mathematics, physics, and chemistry. At the beginning of a two-year study, students were asked to rate their interest in later studying science. Several times over a period of two years teachers were asked to rank their students' interests in science. The ranking of the girls worsened over time.

Girls and boys were asked to rate how much they liked doing a variety of mathematical-physical and linguistic-literary tasks. Mathematical-physical tasks included finding variations of solutions to problems, solving especially difficult tasks, creating tasks by oneself, doing puzzles, and playing chess. Linguistic-literary tasks included making puns; following dialogues in literature, drama, or a radio play; having discussions with intellectuals; and finding contradictions or inconsistencies in texts. The results showed that girls are interested in a variety of areas and that they tend to concentrate their studying in all subjects or content areas rather than investing in one at the expense of the others, as boys tended to do. Over time, girls' interests expanded while boys' interests narrowed.

Classroom Applications

On average, girls often seem not to be as motivated in science and math as boys while achievement or grades might be equal to or better than boys as a group. This phenomenon does not happen because girls have less talent in science than boys. It is because of their greater interest in a wide range of other topics. Consequently, girls will be more easily motivated if science and math concepts touch a wider range of subjects. A greater context and relevance helps students develop a better framework in which to place content-specific facts and concepts.

Most specific curricular content does not exist without a more general context or relevance that touches a range of related issues. For example, try going beyond the book facts to make these connections:

• Relate the structure of the atom or radioactivity to Madame Curie and women's issues she may have experienced during her life.

• Link creativity, discovery, and imagination in arts to creativity in science and other areas where this type of thinking is important.

• Connect creative writing to surrealist painting and the beginnings of psychoanalytical thought and brain research during the same time period.

• Relate the development of technology to sociology or human history. What role did technology play within the social and cultural constructs at specific times in history? You might have students work on projects that correspond with their interests and write papers or reports.

Precautions and Possible Pitfalls

Don't be disappointed if your efforts to motivate girls do not produce observable desired effects. For older girls, entrenched identities tend to have been set in the younger grades. Continue to give all girls the opportunity to demonstrate their abilities to achieve in science. Try narrowing your efforts to a few promising and less resistant girls. A little positive reinforcement and recognition can help. Identify quality work done by girls and have it acknowledged beyond your classroom in the school paper, the science fair, or in student competitions, and so on. Your efforts might plant seeds that will blossom in later years.

Sources

Brickhouse, N., Lowery, P., & Schultz, K. (2000). What kind of girl does science? The construction of school science identities. *Journal of Research in Science Teaching, 37*(5), 441-458.

Pollmer, K. (1991). Was behindert hochbegabte Mädchen, Erfolg im Mathematikunterricht zu erreichen? [What handicaps highly talented girls in being successful in mathematics?] *Psychologie in Erziehung und Unterricht, 38,* 28-36.

Strategy 12: Address gender issues in the classroom. This can increase student success and confidence.

What the Research Says

Research from a study by Good and Brophy (1987) found that teachers give male students greater opportunities to expand ideas and be animated than they do females. In addition, teachers tend to reinforce males for general responses more than they do females. Further, beginning teachers need to be cognizant of the tendency to give more and better feedback to males than to females (Sadker & Sadker, 1994). Previous studies by Fennema and Peterson (1987) state that although female students learn best cooperatively and males learn more easily through competition, it is noteworthy for teachers to give all students opportunities to participate in both learning modes.

Classroom Applications

Before looking further into gender issues, beginning teachers (and veterans too) need to be familiar with Title IX of the 1972 Education Amendments. Title IX forbids discrimination or segregation of students by gender in school programs, courses, or activities. Most people familiar with Title IX think of its legislative implications as specifically to support equal opportunities for girls in sports. The reality is that the law provides equal opportunities for girls *and* boys at school.

Teachers need to examine their own biases with regard to gender differences and the ways this attitude might affect their teaching. Having a colleague observe class while keeping track of the number of times female students versus male students are called on, whether the interaction is different with boys than with girls, and what types of questions and instructional strategies are used with girls as compared to boys are all helpful ways to bring biases to the forefront and to find ways to improve. Videotaping a lesson might also help a teacher practice and polish new instructional strategies.

One way to provide opportunities for success is to provide learning strategies for all students. For example, to make sure every student has equal opportunities to answer questions in class, the teacher could have 3×5" cards with a student's name printed on each card. During a question and answer session, the teacher can shuffle the cards and draw out a card. The teacher then calls on the name of the student on that card to answer the question. Once the student answers the question or verbally participates in a discussion, the teacher can make a mark on the card to record that student's participation. This same system can be used to assign students to cooperative learning groups as well as to assign specific roles within that group (investigator, recorder, etc.).

Teachers should find guest speakers from both genders and from diverse populations. Females and males in nontraditional roles can become role models for students as well as help them see themselves in those careers in the future.

Teachers need to experiment with and implement those strategies that are sensitive to the caliber and equality of interaction with each student, that provide occasions for every student to participate actively in his or her own learning, and to build opportunities for all students to take leadership roles.

Sources

Fennema, E., & Peterson, P. (1987). Effective teaching for girls and boys: The same or different. In D. C. Berliner & B. V. Rosenshine (Eds.), *Talks to teachers* (pp. 11-125). New York: Random House

Good, T. L., & Brophy, J. E. (1987). *Looking in classrooms.* New York: Harper & Row.

Sadker, M., & Sadker, D. (1994). *Failing at fairness: How America's schools cheat girls.* New York: Scribners.

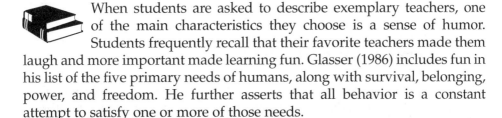

Strategy 13: Add humor to student interactions. Sprinkle classroom time and all student encounters with a little humor.

What the Research Says

When students are asked to describe exemplary teachers, one of the main characteristics they choose is a sense of humor. Students frequently recall that their favorite teachers made them laugh and more important made learning fun. Glasser (1986) includes fun in his list of the five primary needs of humans, along with survival, belonging, power, and freedom. He further asserts that all behavior is a constant attempt to satisfy one or more of those needs.

It is no secret that teachers who engage students have found the use of humor as a positive way of putting students at ease, gaining attention, and showing students that the teacher is indeed human.

According to Quina (1989), if teachers and students can laugh together, they can most likely work together as well. In these days of standards and high-stakes accountability, if students are comfortable and enjoy the learning process, they are more likely to remember more of the material presented.

Csikszentmihalyi and McCormack (1995) indicate that only after a student has learned to love learning does education truly begin. What student doesn't reflect fondly on a teacher who used stories, analogies, or amusing anecdotes to enhance learning and aid in the retention of knowledge?

Classroom Applications

Humor does not simply mean telling jokes. Humor involves putting a positive spin on reality. Negative humor deals with sarcasm and cynicism, which is never appropriate in the classroom. The teacher who uses humor in a positive way models for students a better way to deal with everyday adverse situations, teaches students not to take small crises and assignments too seriously, and creates a more welcoming atmosphere.

In addition, humor helps a student deal with stress, can enhance his or her self-image, and counteract unhappiness, depression, and anxiety. It can stimulate creative and flexible thinking, facilitate learning, and improve interest and attention in the classroom.

Humor can be an extremely useful tool in building rapport. A teacher who can laugh at himself or herself, and can laugh with (but never at) students, can help establish a positive, inviting classroom climate.

The use of humor can do a lot to generate interest and grab a reluctant student's attention. The teacher who dresses up as Lincoln to deliver the Gettysburg Address, or who has students write and perform a rap song to learn the endocrine system and its functions, will make the information presented memorable for the students.

One of the many characteristics of a good teacher is to aid students as they become active learners. A goal of many teachers is to have students enjoy not only the class, but also the subject matter. Humor can help achieve this goal.

Precautions and Possible Pitfalls

The teacher must be careful not to use inappropriate humor that could be offensive or sarcastic or that makes references to ethnic, racial, religious, or gender differences. This type of humor is totally inappropriate in the classroom and is almost always at the expense of other students. The teacher must also be sensitive to cultural differences as well as age-appropriate humor. It is important for each teacher to find a distinct style of humor. If teachers are not comfortable with using humor, they can start off slowly with reading a funny quip or quote. One veteran teacher, knowing her lesson would involve extensive lecturing that day, used an overhead cartoon when students complained they had been sitting for a long time. The text stated, "The mind can hold only what the seat can endure."

Sources

Csikzentmihalyi, M., & McCormack, J. (1995). The influence of teachers. In K. Ryan & J. Cooper (Eds.), *Kaleidoscope: Readings in education* (pp. 2-8). Boston: Houghton Mifflin.

Glasser, W. (1986). *Control theory in the classroom.* New York: Harper & Row.

Quina, J. (1989). *Effective secondary teaching: Going beyond the bell curve.* New York: Harper & Row.

Strategy 14: Reduce the emotional distances between you and your students.

What the Research Says

This research describes the conceptual framework, methodology, results, and ideas from a project on the "Emotions of Teaching and Educational Change" (Hargreaves, 2000). Drawing upon interviews with 53 teachers in 15 schools, the paper describes key differences in the emotional closeness and levels of interaction between elementary and secondary teaching.

The study found that secondary school teaching is characterized by greater professional and physical distance from students, leading teachers to often treat emotions and emotional involvement as intrusions into the classroom and teacher-student relationships. As a result, teachers and students rarely share emotional goals or develop emotional bonds or connections. This means, according to the researchers, that secondary teachers may not feel that they are known by their students as moral, emotional, and caring people. Teachers are then stereotyped and emotional misunderstandings develop. Students see teachers without a real-life context or personality.

Teachers often are responsive to students' emotions only when these emotions might interfere with students' learning. In most classrooms, emotions are noticed only when they force a departure from what is developmentally and academically "normal." This notion is often in conflict with the elementary teaching and learning environment where emotional connections are more the norm. These situations are often exasperated by high school and middle school students who have four or more teachers a day and the same number of content or subject areas. Teachers are more concerned about fending off and managing negative emotions that threaten to intrude from the outside rather than developing positive emotions in their own right. A secondary teacher often will develop and build more meaningful relationships with students outside of classes (extracurricular activities). Outside the class they build a more solid base of understanding on which successful teaching can be built.

The study also found that the many current forms of curricular reform reinforce fragmented interactions between teachers and their students as cognitive content coverage is the focus. Standardized testing contributes to this. This makes personal understanding and personal knowledge and acknowledgment difficult to achieve. The study concludes with the statement that if we are serious about standards, we must become serious about emotions too. We must look again at the organizational conditions and professional expectations that can increase emotional understanding between teachers and students. The researchers argue that emotional connections contribute to educational goals and student achievement and should be included in curriculum reform and pedagogical strategies.

Classroom Applications

Most secondary school teachers see more than 90 students a day and are expected to try to meet all their needs. Content curricular goals are the focus and emotional and personal connections with students often take a backseat. However, if teachers look at their own careers as students, they will find that the teachers remembered most are those who formed some personal emotional bond with the student. The student found himself or herself working harder for that teacher. Teachers need to take time to know their students, which can seem risky for new teachers when coverage of subject matter seems so important. Focusing on or emphasizing content or subject matter alone can limit the effectiveness of a good teacher. First, coverage doesn't ensure learning has taken place. Second, curricular coverage only works if students care about what the teacher has to say. There has to be buy-in and engagement. It is true that to teach students, you must first reach them.

Consider the following argument for nurturing a more collegial, emotionally friendly learning environment. Today some reform philosophies compare the act of athletic coaching to classroom teaching pedagogy. Coaches generally know their players to a greater degree than most teachers know their students. They are aware of individual and team mood swings. They know when to motivate and when to back off. The coaches read the needs of their teams and players and design pathways and strategies to properly train team members. Coverage doesn't work here when or if players need more specific help.

By taking more of a coaching perspective, teachers will see their students in a more personal, caring style. They will form a more collegial teaching and learning environment and create opportunities for closer emotional connections.

Additionally, extracurricular activities are increasingly coached or led by "walk-ons" or people from the community. Teacher-coaches are becoming more rare. A new teacher should try working with students outside the formal classroom. Students will begin to know the teacher better, and the teacher's reputation as a "person" will filter through the student body. If you have a passion for a sport or other activity, think about sharing your enthusiasm with your students.

Another way to better connect to students, especially students who present unique problems, is to network with other teachers who share them. Often other teachers can provide insight into a student's performance. As new teachers learn more about what their students' interests are, they will gain a more informed perspective with regard to how to deal with them. Teachers can also share strategies and reinforce each other's efforts.

Precautions and Possible Pitfalls

Like the expectations teachers have for their students, students have expectations for their teachers. Some students have come to expect a less personal connection and simply aren't interested in forming more complex relationships with their teachers. They like remaining academically anonymous. The beginning teacher will have to learn when to accept this and when to back off. This holds true for parent relationships also. Some parents want to be involved and others don't. The new teacher shouldn't take a lack of involvement personally.

Also, the teacher should be careful about coming across in a too contrived manner. The new teacher should be sincere in his or her efforts and should try to work within his or her own personality, rather than trying to develop a new one just for teaching.

Source

Hargreaves, A. (2000). Mixed emotions: Teachers' perceptions of their interactions with students. *Teaching and Education, 16,* 811-826.

2

Managing
Classroom
Organization
and Discipline

 Strategy 15: Recruit a teaching partner as a peer coach. Choosing a partner at your site and arranging a peer coaching collaboration can help foster your pedagogical skills and competencies.

What the Research Says

In this study, the effects of peer coaching procedures were analyzed. In this case reciprocal peer coaching is described as teachers observing one another and exchanging support, companionship, feedback, and assistance in a coequal or nonthreatening fashion. Peer coaching is designed to foster a teacher's development and acclimation during periods of the development and introduction of new instructional practices in the classroom. This is in contrast to the traditional methods of staff development that rely on one-shot inservice training. Districts that inaugurate fundamental changes in the ways that teachers work, learn, and interact are also presumed to be more effective in addressing students' learning needs and capacities (Firestone & Bader, 1992; Little, 1990).

In this case, four teachers planned and conducted instructional innovation during the study on peer coaching relationships. They mixed and matched, completing the instructional planning and tasks both independently and with peer coaching. Outcomes measured the focus of teachers' collaboration with a peer coach, each teacher's procedural practices and refinements, a variety of student and teacher processes, and the teachers' ongoing concerns and satisfaction with the innovation. They found the following:

● Three stages of different levels of need were identified as distinctive. Not surprisingly, they occur in a longitudinal fashion in Year 1 through Year 3. The first stage is described as survival, where teachers question their competence and desire to become teachers. Assistance takes the form of reassurance and specific skills almost on a daily basis as new teachers adapt to the transition into schools. In the second year, teachers have entered into a consolidation stage that focuses on instruction and the needs of individual students. In the third stage of renewal, teachers have become competent. Previously adopted activities and patterns have become routine and in some cases are not very challenging. In this stage teachers are looking for new ideas in their specialization.

● Teachers working independently make few changes or refinements to their innovations. They made more changes and procedural refinements during peer coaching.

● Many of the changes were sustained and reinforced in peer tutoring arrangements.

● In a related study (Sparks & Bruder, 1987), it was found that 70% of the teachers who participated in coaching felt that their newly developed peer coaching technique produced marked improvement in students' academic skills and competencies.

● Some educators have suggested that peer coaching and reciprocal learning help avoid isolation and foster communication, trust, and support. In this way it helps alleviate potential burnout.

● Peer coaching provided promising solutions, enabling teachers to develop and tailor innovations to fit their personal teaching styles and needs at their site.

From a minority perspective, it was reported that some teachers felt it was a violation of traditional norms of autonomy, privacy, and equality in schools. Overall, the findings of the study support peer coaching strategies and suggest further refinement to help with some of the concerns voiced during the study.

Classroom Applications

Peer coaching works. If it has not been a part of your teacher education program, arrange your own relationships. There is ample academic and professional literature on many versions of the technique. There are also many versions of these arrangements that can evolve into team teaching or integrated or cooperative learning when teachers from different content areas share the same students and a similar curriculum or pedagogy.

Students involved in such relationships often feel much less isolated as teachers begin to know them well. It shrinks the size of the school as teachers team together and share students and support each other's curriculum and instructional practices.

Many of these relationships begin informally; new teachers need to be open to these opportunities. Occasionally they are mandated. Whichever way you go, you need to know that effective collaboration can take practice and acclimation. New teachers may need to put their nervousness aside and go into this relationship feeling a little uncomfortable. Consider teaming with another new teacher.

A little background research can also help you find new ways to use peer coaching as you see how others use it in their settings.

Precautions and Possible Pitfalls

Peer coaching can take time. Instead of doing grades or a million other things, the new teacher will need to be available to observe and plan with others. If this is a problem, consider peer relationships for a single unit or lesson and then move on. Teachers don't need to sustain peer coaching beyond its usefulness. Come together only when it is logical and practical.

Sources

Firestone, W. A., & Bader, B. D. (1992). *Redesigning teaching: Professionalism or bureaucracy?* Albany: State University of New York.

Kohler, F. W., Crilley, K. M., Shearer, D. D., & Good, G. (1997). Effects of peer coaching on teacher and student outcomes. *Journal of Educational Research, 90*(4), 240.

Little, J. W. (1990). Norms of collegiality and experimentation: Workplace conditions of school success. *American Education Research Journal, 19,* 325-340.

Sparks, G., & Bruder, S. (1987). Before and after peer coaching. *Educational Leadership, 3,* 54-57.

 ### Srategy 16: Share your discipline-related problems with a colleague. This will help reduce your stress.

What the Research Says

Of all the activities that make up the job description of a teacher, classroom discipline is one of, if not the most, significant. Discipline can be distinguished from the broader area of classroom management in that the latter emphasizes the provision of quality instruction as a means of limiting disruption in instruction whereas discipline is generally represented as what teachers do in response to students' misbehavior. It is the gap that exists between the discipline procedures used by the teacher and his or her idea of the best or better practice. This research looks at the tensions that arise from a teacher's desire to use educationally justifiable models of discipline while still quickly gaining and maintaining order in the classroom. It examines the resulting stress that arises when teachers are unable to discipline the students as they would ideally prefer. The results indicate that teachers who report more stress are those most interested in empowering their students in the decision-making process. The most concerned teachers indicated a greater range of worry, self-blame, tension, wishful thinking, and self-isolation. There was also an indication of a greater tendency for these teachers to get sick as a result of the stress.

Institutional pressure also contributes to a teacher's choice of a discipline plan that they might not choose themselves. This can be especially true for new teachers. Many times a beginning teacher is forced to employ a variety of coping strategies, both public and personal. Tensions can and do exist between personal philosophy and institutionally preferred teacher-student interaction. Beginning teachers often seek the privacy and isolation of their rooms to negotiate a management role that works for them. Their results sometimes remain minimally acceptable from an institutional perspective.

In this case a survey was conducted to assess teachers' level of concern about discipline. Questionnaires were administered to half of all teachers in a sample of 15 government-regulated secondary schools in Melbourne, Australia.

The study found and suggested that teachers generally cope productively with the stress of being unable to produce self-defined best practices in the area of classroom discipline. They claim it was also clear that those teachers who are most stressed are more likely to include in their coping management skills maladaptive strategies which contribute to and help maintain high levels of stress. This may be happening because the dysfunctional strategies undermine or negate the benefits that accrue from the use of more adaptive strategies such as setting clear expectations and creating a less confrontational focus. Most important, the results stress that teachers experiencing the greatest amounts of discipline problems make matters worse by not letting others know about their concerns and suffering in silence.

Classroom Applications

To begin, it can be argued that even when student misbehavior disrupts a teacher's attempt to instruct students, the teacher's level of stress is reduced and coping mechanisms are enhanced when the teacher feels part of a professional school community. New teachers tend to suffer in silence for fear of appearing weak or unable to control their classes. Both experienced teachers and teachers in a school new to them face problems site-established teachers don't.

The students predisposed to misbehaving will test the teacher and the teacher's management and discipline policies to an extent greater than established colleagues at the site. Some students will attempt to transfer responsibility for their grades or failures onto the teacher and they will tell their parents it is the teacher's fault. This is not to say that students are always wrong and the teacher is always right. A teacher's policies very well might be out of that school's paradigm of acceptable practice and what the students are familiar with. Chances are the teacher is not too far off, but not knowing what colleagues are doing may make the new teacher feel insecure. However, if a teacher is having problems with specific classes or students,

• Avoid new-teacher management and discipline problems by networking with site-experienced teachers before school starts. Adjust personal policies as necessary to fit the situation and specific student groups.

• Share your classroom management and discipline policies with the students early. Adjust and fine-tune them after receiving student input. Have students sign the rules, thereby acknowledging their existence and their understanding of them. Collect them and file these signed documents. Students are more reluctant to break rules when they have signed and formally acknowledged them. This procedure also begins a discipline paper trail.

• Listen to students' concerns. Try not to argue your points in front of the class unless you have already established a relationship of trust with students. Work with individuals privately so as not to provide that misbehaving student with an audience.

• Bounce the situation off a colleague, counselor, or administrator. Take advice and be ready to mitigate, litigate, or compromise. You may find that the students have valid points. Reduce the tension of the situation by negotiation. The teacher may also need to acknowledge a student's concerns and stand his or her ground. Focus on the problems, not the emotional part of the situation.

• Prepare a backup plan. What is the next step to be taken? If it is to present the issue to counselors or administrators, talk to them early and let them know the problem is coming. If they know the students and the parents, they can often suggest strategies for home communication. Again, listen to their suggestions.

• Teachers need to be prepared to learn from their mistakes and fine-tune management and discipline policies for the next class or school year.

• Don't suffer in isolation! New teachers often see management problems as personal weaknesses that they want to hide from evaluators and others. A willingness to adjust, adapt, and listen and learn from others helps alleviate the feeling of isolation. A clearly visible relationship with other professionals on campus tells students that the new teacher is in the loop and is supported by other established educators. Have counselors, exemplary colleagues, or administrators visit your classes. Get comfortable working while in the proximity of colleagues.

Precautions and Possible Pitfalls

Most schools have discipline management policies that are designed to leave a paper trail. Most of the time classroom management and discipline policies work and you never need documentation. However, every so often, a student doesn't respond, and the teacher will need to document the disciplinary process taken. Sometimes teachers wait too long, hoping the student will come around before starting the paper trail. Knowing when to formally document discipline and bring others into the mix is something a new teacher learns with experience. However, there is usually a point where your system fails to remedy a discipline problem. Your system may work for 95% of the students, but some just don't respond. At that point, it is a good time to bring in support and be ready to document what you have done up to that point.

Sources

Bullough, R. V. (1994). Digging at the roots: Discipline, management and metaphor. *Action in Teacher Education, 16*(1), 1-10.

Lewis, R. (1999). Teachers coping with the stress of classroom discipline. *Social Psychology of Education, 3,* 155-171.

Strategy 17: Become knowledgeable about youth culture. This will help you successfully engage students.

What the Research Says

It is no secret that some of the most difficult challenges facing beginning teachers are classroom management, physical and emotional isolation, and difficulty adapting to the needs and abilities of their students.

Brock and Grady (1997) concluded, "Teaching is one of the few careers in which the least experienced members face the greatest challenges and responsibilities" (p. 11). Many beginning teachers come prepared with book knowledge and theory, but the reality of controlling a classroom of 35 students is a whole other story. This reality usually hits after the first few weeks of school when the honeymoon period is over for the students and they have figured out what they can and can't get away with in a particular class.

In many teacher preparation, induction, and mentoring programs across the nation, these issues are being addressed with concrete solutions and qualified mentors. Connecting with exemplary veteran teachers with experience and rapport with adolescents can also be a big help. New teachers at the secondary level report their teacher colleagues having a positive influence in helping them understand the challenges of adolescents. Conversely, elementary teachers felt their principals were extremely helpful in providing support and encouragement.

Classroom Applications

No longer can we tolerate a "sink or swim" attitude. In California, the BTSA (Beginning Teacher Support and Assessment) program focuses in on the beginning teacher learning as much as possible about the students in their classrooms. Knowing which languages are spoken at home, previous student test scores, the community in which these students live, and cultural and socioeconomic background all help the novice teacher understand and adapt to the needs of the students they teach. Check literature, music, clothing trends, and so on. Spend time looking over popular magazines, check on students' favorite films and television shows, and most important take time to talk to and *listen* to kids.

Precautions and Possible Pitfalls

With the social climate today and students coming to class with a myriad of challenges and concerns, it is more important than ever for teachers to be aware of the problems and challenges of adolescent culture. What may seem trivial to an adult can be monumental to an adolescent. Students would rather be considered "bad" in front of their peers than "stupid." Yet many times a novice teacher will put students in the position of acting out because they don't know the answer to a question. Be careful not to judge students based on what other teachers say. All students deserve teachers who have not made up their minds on what the students are capable of in the classroom. Be careful of becoming too much of a "buddy" or "friend"—not retaining adult status, modeling adult ideas and behavior. The more a teacher can invest in understanding the students, where they are coming from, and what is important to them, the more successful the teacher can be in implementing classroom management procedures.

Sources

Brock, B. L., & Grady, M. L. (1997). *From first-year to first-rate: Principals guiding beginning teachers.* Thousand Oaks, CA: Corwin.

Lortie, D. C. (1975). *Schoolteacher: A sociological study.* Chicago: University of Chicago.

Strategy 18: Save your voice by engaging students in curricular conversations. Just because you're the teacher doesn't mean you have to do all the talking.

What the Research Says

Several recent studies suggest that teachers experience a higher frequency of voice-strain symptoms (67%) as compared with nonteachers (33%), regardless of their age (Smith, Gray, Dove, Kirchner, & Heras, 1997). On average a teacher talks for 6.3 hours during a typical school day (Siebert, 1999). In another study of more than 1,000 teachers, it was found that almost 21% had a pathological voice condition (Urrutikoetzea, Ispizua, & Matellanes, 1995).

Classroom Applications

With teachers using their voices all day, lecturing, answering questions, giving instructions, and sometimes even yelling, the constant strain on their vocal cords can lead to an increase in teacher absenteeism. New teachers frequently raise their voices as a way of compensating for noisy or disruptive students. When students are talking in competition with the teacher, the first thing a novice teacher might do is raise his or her voice to either get students' attention or to drown out student raucousness. Add to this situation classrooms with loud ventilation systems, poor insulation between classrooms, and outside sources such as automobile traffic and aircraft overhead, and it's no wonder teachers' voices become strained.

A resolution to this is the paradox "less is more." One of the most effective classroom management techniques in dealing with noisy or disruptive students is to actually reduce the volume of the teacher's voice to almost a whisper. This technique forces the student(s) to stop talking to be able to hear the teacher speaking. Often teachers fall into the trap of raising their voices sometimes to the point of yelling, a technique not generally considered effective in the long run. Many new teachers believe a louder voice will restore order. This tactic may work in the short term, but soon students will just tune out. A far more effective method is for the teacher to stop talking completely until the student or class is quiet. The obvious statement from beginning teachers is, "If I stop talking and teaching every time a student is talking out of turn, I'll never get the lesson taught." This is simply not the case. If a student or the class is talking or disruptive, they aren't listening to what the teacher is saying anyway. Teachers end up repeating instructions multiple times, losing valuable classroom time. Students will quickly learn that instruction stops when students aren't attentive. The key is for the teacher to resist the urge to shush students or to immediately return to talking once the noise begins to abate. Students need to learn early that instruction will stop and the focus of the lesson will not continue until everyone is quiet and paying attention. For the teacher this refrain from talking may seem like minutes, but, in actuality, it's usually only 15 to 20 seconds of wait time before the class is quiet.

Teachers often think that if they aren't talking then they aren't teaching. Beginning teachers should explore ways in which to give directions without using verbal instructions. Teachers can write directions on the chalkboard or put them on an overhead transparency. Another way to prevent voice strain is to establish procedures such as an agenda that is posted (to stop the 20 "what are we going to do today?" questions). Teachers should have procedures in place for turning in homework, passing papers, asking a question, or getting into groups that don't require their voice. With younger students, hand signals or a bell might signal it's time to get into groups.

Precautions and Possible Pitfalls

When it comes to teaching we need to remember the axiom "work smarter, not harder." Frequently new teachers forget that there are other ways of delivering the lesson besides direct instruction. With the short attention spans of students (of all ages), teachers need to explore alternative ways of instruction. A teacher's voice is an important instrument in teaching and care should be taken to preserve it.

Sources

Siebert, M. (1999, February 7). Educators often struck by voice ailments. *The Des Moines Register*, 4.

Smith, E., Gray, S. D., Dove, H., Kirchner, L., & Heras, H. (1997). Frequency and effects of teachers' voice problems. *Journal of Voice, 11*(1), 81-87.

Urrutikoetzea, A., Ispizua, A., & Matellanes, F. (1995). Vocal pathology in teachers: A video-laryngostroboscopic study of 1,046 teachers. *Rev Laryngology, Otology, Rhinology, 116*(4), 255-262.

3

Managing Classroom Time

 Strategy 19: Manage the special challenges within block scheduling. Teachers new to block or modified block scheduling need to give special attention to the challenges that longer class periods present to their curriculum and pedagogy.

What the Research Says

The purpose of this study was to examine the experiences of new teachers as they negotiated the beginning of their career in less traditional schedules. In this case a new teacher was described as a teacher less than three months out of their teacher preparation program. The study lasted one calendar year and included 31 first-year teachers. Data were collected from these teachers in three urban school districts that had high schools offering a 4 × 4 block schedule. Data were collected from the first-year teachers only and did not include administrators, master teachers, and other support staff.

Three areas emerged as problematic:

- Adjusting instruction to extended class period formats
- Transitioning learning activities
- Assessing student progress

In the adjustment category, the problems identified included managing class time, varying instruction throughout the class period, running out of materials or activities before the end of class, and relying on only a single instructional method.

Many fell into patterns of worksheets or end of chapter questions, long lectures, or letting students do homework to keep them quiet until the bell. First-year teachers were not prepared to vary instructional strategies or make transitions. Some resorted to college-type teaching, heavy on notes and lecture.

Transition periods from one activity to another, using a variety of instructional strategies that are desirable in a block format, became a sticking point for new teachers. Maintaining a learning environment and climate became difficult and students "messed around too much" or saw it as a time to misbehave. Because of this, new teachers often avoided transition periods and used only limited numbers of instructional strategies. Teachers in the study often reported being very uncomfortable with students out of their seats or moving around. "Losing control" became a very limiting fear in the creation of learning environments.

This fear also limited assessment strategies and tactics. Many new teachers found pencil and paper tests could not adequately assess gains in student learning. Yet, performance assessments were rare because of, again, the fear of losing control. Thus "seat work" became the norm. Socratic seminars, cooperative learning strategies, simulations, role-playing, laboratory, or work-station strategies presented management problems that most new teachers were not equipped to deal with. New teachers often had problems knowing how much value or weight to place on more authentic assessments and "doing" types of activities. They did not realize that alternative forms of assessment could be quantified by criteria matched to learning objectives through rubrics.

Longer class periods require careful, structured planning, use of a variety of instructional methods, and diverse assessment practices to maximize the potential they offer. New teachers "on the block" and especially first-year teachers had problems fully developing skills in these areas. The study also found that if the staff-development opportunities were beyond the range of the first-year teachers, learning advanced techniques created frustration for the teachers that transferred to the classroom.

Classroom Applications

If, as a new or preservice teacher, one should anticipate teaching in a block schedule format, consider the results of this study. Most, if not all, schools that use a block or modified block schedule also favor a student-centered curricular approach to student learning or pedagogy. It is also clear new teachers often encounter discipline and management problems when students leave their seats. Unfortunately, experience is often the best teacher. For new teachers, their student-teaching experience might have been very different than what they may be facing in their first teaching position. So what can a teacher do?

There are many terms within educational jargon that describe teaching and learning arrangements better suited for the longer timeframes typical of block schedules.

The concepts of problem-based, theme-based, student-centered, or activity and discovery learning ask students to take a more active role in their own learning. Teachers facilitate or orchestrate learning rather than dictate it. Ted Sizer's (of Brown University) Coalition of Essential Schools philosophy sees the student as a worker and the teacher as a facilitator. The point here is that students are required to take a more proactive role in their own learning, when they need to know things and what they need to know. These types of teaching and learning arrangements also require the students to learn a new role and you to teach students their new role. Many students have not learned to self-regulate in classrooms that teach in a student-centered manner.

Successful student-centered classroom environments in block formats often look chaotic but are actually highly planned and organized chaos. The most important idea to keep in mind is to teach students to learn in these new settings. Most kids coming from the "stand-and-deliver" experience are not equipped to deal with the new expectations in longer classes. So between your inexperience and their inexperience you must realize that it will require time, usually a semester to a year, for both you and the students to adjust.

Teachers can help themselves by learning all they can about how to create, manage, and assess and evaluate activity-based classes (typical of block schedules) and activities. Every activity and expected student or curricular outcome needs to be broken down into smaller manageable units with built-in student accountability at each step along the way. How small the teacher makes these subunits depends on the maturity and educational needs of the students being managed. The pace of instruction needs to be flexible and the teacher needs to expect to make adjustments on the fly as the students give clues that they're not getting it or as the teacher runs into curricular roadblocks. Every student moves at a different pace.

When administrators come into a class the teacher needs to be accountable. Teachers should be prepared to tout their latest student-based activity and show the administrator how they manage the learning that is taking place. Have an administrator shadow an activity or a student through that activity. Any administrator in a block schedule type school knows what the teacher is up against and can often offer help or direct the new teacher to a teacher who could be helpful. The sooner the administrators see the new teachers are engaged in trying to make the best of their schedules, the sooner the teachers will receive support.

Precautions and Possible Pitfalls

 Student-centered learning and block scheduling does not mean a teacher needs to abandon all stand-and-deliver or other more traditional techniques. To completely abandon techniques a teacher is experienced with or has learned and add a whole new set of methods is a ticket for frustration and potential disaster. Teachers should plan to step out of their comfort zone, but not completely. Planning short-term units, using unfamiliar strategies, acclimating slowly, and tinkering and modifying as you go may be more effective with a new teacher. Eventually new teaching and learning methods will take over or blend with the teacher's existing methods. Again, teachers are learning on their feet and this takes time.

If new teachers are trying another teacher's strategy or activity, they should expect to need to modify it to fit their own comfort zone. And finally, stepping into a new position needs to be seen as a work in progress. A teacher should plan full acclimation as a two- or three-year experience.

Source

Zepeda, S. J., & Mayers, R. S. (2001, April/May). New kids on the block: Beginning teachers face challenges. *High School Journal, 84*(4), 1-11.

 Strategy 20: Become a classroom manager before becoming a content specialist.

What the Research Says

Teacher planning refers to the wide variety of instructional decisions teachers make prior to the execution of plans during teaching. Some of the key factors found to affect planning practices include students, curriculum materials, teacher guides, and the physical facilities. In the student realm, ability level, gender, amount of class participation, student self-concepts, social competence, and work habits contribute to many other planning considerations. Curriculum materials influence decisions based on the quality or quantity of textbooks and support materials. The physical facilities include room size and a variety of other related school characteristics that include the all-important school schedule. The goals of the administration, site administrators, and school and department policies also add to the many considerations teachers face. To these external forces add the teacher's own interests, subject matter specialty, and experience.

This study (Sardo-Brown, 1996) looked into the literature and found few studies that looked at novice teacher planning. Sardo-Brown's study looked at how two first-year teachers planned their first and second years of teaching and compared and contrasted the differences between the years. The two teachers in the study were selected based on their competency within their graduating education classes and because both had obtained employment in secondary schools right out of teacher education.

Some of the most noticeable findings between first- and second-year planning include:

• A clear trend with the idea that they did not plan to emphasize content during the early weeks of school, but considered management issues a higher priority.

• Both second-year novices dedicated much more time to how to set up and teach rules, procedures, and class structure along with how to develop early rapport with their students.

• The teachers moved further away in time and reference from their student-teaching experiences where rules were routinized and planning was rule-bound.

• In the second year, they were more receptive to new ideas and inservicing.

• Both planned major adjustments to their methods of assessment. Both sought out more time-efficient strategies and planned to use more high-level assessment strategies as learning devices.

• Both novices in this study married between their first and second years and looked for new ways to get more leisure time. Both credited their marriages for growing confidence in themselves as teachers and both felt "older."

• In the second year, they tried to do more of their planning at school.

• Both viewed the area of assessment as a major concern and planned numerous changes in their second year. They felt they were not prepared to successfully tackle assessment in their first year.

- **Both felt more comfortable planning in their second year.**

- **Both continued to struggle with the problem of reconciling their own beliefs about their teaching with the incongruent beliefs of the principal and other colleagues.**

- **They both had a greater awareness of the cognitive and emotional needs of their students.**

Classroom Applications

It is clear from the research that preservice teachers move from content specialists and borrowers of instructional tactics to educators and instructional strategists their second year and thereafter. First-year teachers often don't know what they don't know until experience becomes their teacher. The tactic derived from the research is being able to learn from what teachers see in front of them rather than from what someone tells them.

New teachers should develop their own analytical skills as they implement a "best guess" instructional plan. Teachers need to do the "science" it takes to determine what happens when real students meet a teacher's management and instructional strategy. Seeing everything a new teacher does as a work in progress will be comforting. Keep in mind that a teaching style is something new teachers will find in themselves and not something they learn. The classroom experience is like the game on Friday night. It tells the teachers what they need to work on the following week.

Teachers will do well to also remember they are standing on the shoulders of those that came before, and they all went through similar experiences. How beginning teachers view themselves as teachers should not be based solely on early efforts. It should be based on how teachers respond to that effort and reflection and how resilient and adaptive they can be. Analyze those problems, adjust, and move on.

Precautions and Possible Pitfalls

Don't panic! It's clear from the research that time on task is a large factor in one's development as a teacher. For most veterans there are few shortcuts from the first days in class to the beginning of the second year. Holding off on career reflections for the time being and focusing on how students can be helped should be a priority. New teachers will gradually become less concerned with how others see them and more concerned with their students and how teachers can help them as time passes.

Source

Sardo-Brown, D. (1996). A longitudinal study of novice secondary teachers' planning: Year two. *Teaching & Teacher Education, 12*(5), 519-530.

Strategy 21: Learn to multitask.

What the Research Says

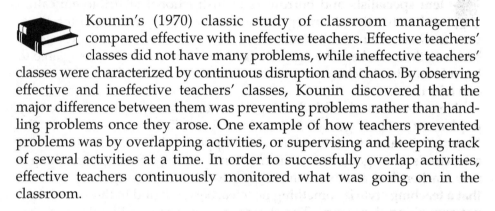

Kounin's (1970) classic study of classroom management compared effective with ineffective teachers. Effective teachers' classes did not have many problems, while ineffective teachers' classes were characterized by continuous disruption and chaos. By observing effective and ineffective teachers' classes, Kounin discovered that the major difference between them was preventing problems rather than handling problems once they arose. One example of how teachers prevented problems was by overlapping activities, or supervising and keeping track of several activities at a time. In order to successfully overlap activities, effective teachers continuously monitored what was going on in the classroom.

Classroom Applications

There is an adage in the teaching world that the teacher needs to continuously move about the classroom and be omnipresent. Proximity to students is a powerful tool. A critical time for the teacher's presence to be made known is at the beginning of a lesson. While students are putting homework problems on an overhead transparency or on the blackboard, the teacher is free to work with individual students. While a teacher or student is collecting homework assignments, the teacher can be introducing the class to the next topic by posing a problem or question to tap and review students' prior knowledge of the topic they will discuss next. While walking around the classroom discussing a topic, a teacher can glance at students' desks to check for homework or to make sure students are looking at the appropriate material. Teachers can also discuss how to solve a problem while walking around and showing their presence to make sure students do not misbehave.

Precautions and Possible Pitfalls

 The key element to bear in mind is for new teachers not to spread themselves too thin when assuming more than one responsibility at a time. Multitasking works best when the results are worthwhile. In addition, teachers shouldn't move around the classroom so much that the movement becomes a distraction for students.

Source

Kounin, J. S. (1970). *Discipline and group management in classrooms.* New York: Holt, Rinehart & Winston.

> *Strategy 22: Post an agenda before the start of class. Provide this overview of the day's lesson on the board or an overhead transparency before the start of class.*

What the Research Says

Using an agenda of the day's lesson makes learning more relevant to students and takes the mystery out of what is going to be covered in class that day. An agenda also helps keep the teacher organized with regard to the information to be learned. An agenda that includes the lesson outline on the board or an overhead transparency can arouse students' thinking about the various topics and help them connect to prior knowledge about those topics. A connection between knowledge already known and new knowledge is a critical component of meaningful learning.

Based on Ausubel's (1960) theory of how knowledge is structured, the most meaningful learning is dependent upon a lesson's material being organized in a way that "connects" and makes it meaningful to the learner. The student needs to be able to connect the information being taught with ideas, concepts, and examples that are already present in the learner's cognitive structure. According to Ausubel, the framework of a preorganized agenda provides a stable sequential structure that students can use as a framework to build upon the objective of the lesson. It prepares students in advance for what is to come, tells students how the teacher has organized the material, and makes the material to be received more meaningful. This process is what Ausubel calls *meaningful reception learning*.

Table 3.1   Sample Agenda

Agenda for: (Subject)   Date:

Homework due:

Review:

New:

Standard addressed:

Next test or project due date:

Homework:

Classroom Applications

Who remembers being in a class and having no idea what was going to be covered that day, whether or not a test was imminent, or if the teacher would assign a hefty homework assignment over a holiday weekend? Most students have had this experience more than once. The use of the board or an overhead transparency covering the day's agenda can serve a number of purposes. The agenda should be posted at the beginning of class, preferably as students are entering the class. Students then know in advance what is to come. It can also cut down or eliminate the number of "what are we going to do today?" questions teachers frequently encounter. There are no surprises about an upcoming assignment, a concept being taught that day, test due dates, or homework assignments. In addition, using an agenda places the onus of responsibility on the students for keeping a record of what material is to be covered not only for themselves but also for students who are absent. Schools which use block scheduling, where students attend class every other day, can benefit even more by not having to wait two days before catching up. The student merely calls a homework buddy, who checks the agenda written down that day. The use of an agenda can alleviate miscommunication problems ("I didn't know we were having a test today") and can reduce the academic stress some students feel while trying to juggle and organize homework, projects, tests, and so on. A sample agenda might include the information shown in Table 3.1. The teacher can easily create these agendas as a computer presentation software slide (e.g., using PowerPoint) and a record is then kept for future planning.

The use of this type of agenda helps keep the teacher focused on the lesson and leaves no secrets for the student about what will be covered that day. By using an overhead transparency, teachers who are assigned to multiple classrooms (not uncommon for a new teacher) are able to take the agenda with them and not waste valuable time rewriting the day's activities in each room. After a lesson, the teacher can use the agenda to make notes about pacing, transitions, and lesson evaluations to be used in subsequent years.

Precautions and Possible Pitfalls

The agenda should not be a detailed outline of each facet of the lesson, but rather a general outline of the day's activities. When students set about copying detailed agendas into notes, their focus turns to note taking, and the teacher risks losing their attention. In addition, agendas should include enough information to pique the student's interest about the day's lesson, but not be so detailed that they become meaningless notes. Copying the agenda should take the student no more than two to three minutes at the beginning of class (allowing the teacher to take attendance, speak with a student, etc.).

Source

Ausubel, D. (1960). The use of advance organizers in the learning and retention of meaningful verbal learning. *Journal of Educational Psychology, 51*, 267-272.

 Strategy 23: Fill in the time by varying instructional strategies within block scheduling, which provides opportunities to use multiple instructional strategies during the same class period.

What the Research Says

A recent study by Benton-Kupper (1999) explored the experiences of three high school teachers in their second year of transition from a traditional six-period per day schedule (45-minute periods) to a block four-period per day schedule (90-minute periods).

Their findings suggest the block schedule provided more opportunities than the traditional six-period day for instructional strategies that actively engage the students in learning. The additional time provided in a double period allows teachers to provide more depth of content within their classroom through discussion, projects, and instructional materials.

Classroom Applications

 For middle and secondary schools across the nation using some type of block scheduling (four 90-minute periods per day, or three 120-minute periods per day, classes meeting every other day), the opportunities abound for teachers to provide time to work individually with students, go deeply into the content, and assess the students' individual learning styles. Teachers at schools where the block schedule has been implemented for many years report that the block increases their ability to know where students are in terms of learning the content. The result of this knowledge allows the teacher to plan and instruct lessons that will lead to student success (Buckman, King, & Ryan 1995).

In a block period there is a tendency for the flow of the lesson to be less disjointed than in a traditional format. Having extended time in a block gives teachers the opportunity to construct a full lesson, introduce a topic or concept, discuss it, and bring that topic to closure all within one class period. Teachers may also find more time in the block schedule to develop difficult key concepts.

In a Southern California high school that has had block scheduling (120-minute periods every other day) for over 25 years, even new teachers find the opportunities to provide a wide range of instructional strategies within a lesson intended to increase students' interest, knowledge, and success. For example, in one class the teacher was able to review for a test, provide direct instruction, have cooperative learning groups, view a video followed by time for a class discussion, and begin individual project presentations, all within the same class period. To be able to cover all these instructional strategies in a traditional class period would be impossible.

The extended timeframe of block scheduling also allows time for activities implementing multiple intelligences that might be more difficult in a nonblock setting.

Teachers also report that with block scheduling there are more opportunities for in-depth reading of literature and class discussions that might not otherwise happen given the relative short 45-minute period. Without this additional time, more work must be assigned as homework, which does not give students the advantage of having the teacher as a facilitator.

Precautions and Possible Pitfalls

New teachers may, at first, be intimidated by the extended time of block scheduling. Their practice in the planning of lessons may be limited to single periods. Concerns about filling the time with worthwhile activities may abound. If they don't have experience in planning for the block, they should consult a trusted colleague or mentor for help in lesson planning. Block scheduling requires a unique perspective. The primary consideration should be to keep students engaged. This can be accomplished by changing activities or focus about every 20 minutes. If students are given the opportunity to experience multiple methods of grasping information, their interest level will be high. The greatest mistake a teacher new to block scheduling can make is to think that lesson planning simply means putting two single-period lessons together. The worst use of the block is for the teacher to present a lecture or lecture-based instruction for the entire class period.

Sources

Benton-Kupper, J. (1999, October). Teaching in the block: Perceptions from within. *High School Journal, 83*(1), 26.

Buckman, D., King, B., & Ryan, S. (1995). Block scheduling: A means to improving school climate. *NASSP Bulletin, 79(571),* 9-18.

4

Organizing
Curricular Goals,
Lesson Plans,
and Instructional
Delivery

 Strategy 24: *Define yourself as a teacher beyond your subject or content knowledge.*

What the Research Says

Knowing lots of information about or within a subject area will not ensure success as a teacher. This research (Kennedy, 1998) raises questions about what math and science teachers need to know to teach math and science well. The study begins by examining reform proposals for K-12 science and math teaching by defining what good teaching practices consist of. It does a literature search to delineate the varieties and types of knowledge that have been associated with this kind of teaching. The focus of the investigation is on subject-matter knowledge, but continues further to address the character of the knowledge rather than the content of the knowledge.

The types of knowledge identified by the research include conceptual understanding of the subject, pedagogical content knowledge beliefs about the nature of work in science and math, attitudes toward the subjects, and actual teaching practices with students.

Unfortunately, the literature is incomplete with respect to which types of this knowledge base are relatively more or less important. Reform commentaries include many ideas about the character of knowledge, beliefs, and attitudes that teachers need to teach math and science in a new, less didactic way. Their comments characterize optimal teacher knowledge as

1. **Conceptual:** having a sense of size and proportion, understanding the central ideas in the discipline, understanding the relationship among ideas, and being able to reason, analyze, and solve problems in the discipline

2. **Pedagogical:** having the ability to generate metaphors and other representations of these ideas based on the knowledge, ability, and experience level of the students

3. **Epistemological:** having an understanding of the nature of work in the disciplines

4. **Attitudinal:** having respect for, and an appreciation of, the processes by which knowledge is generated through the disciplines

There is one important reason, cited in the research, for teachers to possess a rich and deep understanding of their subject knowledge. Reformers want them to stop reciting facts to students and start encouraging students to explore the subject for themselves. Teachers confident in their knowledge can orchestrate this self-discovery with carefully designed teaching strategies and learning pathways.

To carry this idea of literacy further, the way teachers come to understand these proposed forms of discipline-based knowledge are appropriate outcomes not just for teachers but also for college-educated citizens. The limits of the study cite that these characteristics are not clearly understood in the context of actual teaching practices or the way that ideal practice is defined relative to actual practice.

Classroom Applications

 Many individuals new to teaching come with strong content or subject-matter knowledge. Most have majored in a specific area in college or have years of knowledge gathered in the private sector as

professionals. Usually after a few years of teaching, teachers find that content knowledge plays a much smaller role in their success or failure as a teacher than they first thought. While content knowledge is important, it rarely defines your success or failure as a teacher. A teacher not only controls what students will know about a subject but how they come to know it and the context in which it exists.

The research looks into how content or discipline knowledge exists and is defined. It makes a clear distinction between what there is to know and how that material comes to be known. There is much more to know about subject-matter content than just the facts. Evidence suggests that many teachers present their subjects as vast collections of facts, terms, and procedures with little connection among the components. They also present the facts as if they were self-evident and that students should accept and remember them without much thought. If teachers are to engage students in high-level thinking skills, teachers themselves must have a grasp of these ideas (the range of understanding knowledge) and must have a healthy respect for the difficulties of developing and justifying knowledge in their field.

Beyond the basics, a teacher should allow the students to use questions and misconceptions in guiding their exploration of subject matter and the nature of knowing. Be prepared to guide students to clarify confusions and to ensure misconceptions are not perpetuated.

Be aware that some questions or hypotheses are beyond either the teacher's or the students' capacities to pursue or generate ideas and will lead the teacher and the lessons astray, down dead-end alleys, or into trivial pursuits. Teachers are not expected to move in any direction the class might want to go. Teachers learn to manage classroom direction by recognizing which questions or comments might be fruitful and which to stay away from.

Remember that covering just basic knowledge does not guarantee retention or usefulness. Very often it is *how* a person comes to know something that contributes to long-term retention and usefulness. Students must be motivated to guide the direction (curiosity and interest) in which knowledge is dispersed and acquired.

It also helps to keep in mind that knowledge in any discipline has a past, present, and future. Some of learning has a finite shelf life and students need to understand that too.

Precautions and Possible Pitfalls

If teachers are having trouble defining the boundaries of content knowledge, they should begin to consider a new term to add to educational jargon: *recitational* subject-matter knowledge. It refers to the types of knowledge that have traditionally been tested in achievement tests in the past. Recitational knowledge also covers the ability to recite specific facts on demand, to recognize correct answers on multiple-choice tests, to define terms correctly, and to be good test takers. Many reformers think that traditional courses and curricula are limited to recitational knowledge. It is their aim to extend the character of discipline knowledge beyond this point.

Keep in mind that *what* to teach is usually more politically loaded than *how* to teach it or to know it. Also, covering material by incorporating superficial instructional techniques does little for retention. It only provides a false sense of security. Discipline knowledge must include having strategies that the teacher can use to provide context and relevance to recitational knowledge in order to cause true learning to occur.

Sources

American Association for the Advancement of Science. (1989). *Science for all Americans: A Project 2001 report on literacy goals in science, mathematics, and technology.* Washington, DC: Author.

Kennedy, M. (1998). Education reform and subject-matter knowledge. *Journal of Research in Science Teaching, 35*(3), 249-263.

Strategy 25: Remember that less = more and streamline the content of your curriculum. Instead of teaching a broad survey course that covers many topics superficially, focus your course on the most important content in enough depth for students to actually understand, remember, and apply what they have learned.

What the Research Says

Eylon and Linn (1988) report that, cognitively, students respond better to a systematic, in-depth treatment of a few topics than they do to conventional in-breadth treatment of many topics. Increasingly it is recommended that teachers, of all subjects, streamline the curriculum and focus more on a limited set of knowledge and skills. Students' misconceptions and lack of understanding of basics reflect limitations of mental processing and memory. Ted Sizer, a well-known progressive educator, identifies "less is more," as one of the major principles to guide educational reform. For more information, see "Less Is More: The Secret of Being Essential" in *Horace,* the online journal of the Coalition of Essential Schools Web site at www.essentialschools.org.

Classroom Applications

Teachers should examine the course(s) preceding theirs that students must take to get the background for their course and examine the courses following theirs for which students are expected to acquire the background. Teachers may then use this information to identify the key information their course must cover. Once these decisions have been made, a teacher can then eliminate chapters of the textbook from the course to prevent overload and rote learning.

Precautions and Possible Pitfalls

Don't throw out "diamonds in the rough," potentially interesting learning pathways, or favorite topics. There's a lot to be said for the effects of teacher enthusiasm for specific concepts, topics, and content on student motivation. A wise teacher will use them! The teacher just may have less time to spend on them.

Sources

Cushman, K. (1994, November). Less is more: The secret of being essential. *Horace*, *11*(2), 1-4.

Eylon, B., & Linn, M. (1988). Learning and instruction: An examination of four research perspectives in science education. *Review of Educational Research, 58*, 251-301.

Strategy 26: Use state and national standards to establish benchmarks for assessing your students' literacy.

What the Research Says

Research that describes the way that professional development activities use standards is rare or nonexistent. However, academic literature is rich in critical and editorial review. As expected, there is a variety of views presented. They range from the use of standards to produce formula or universally standardized content, processes, and assessments to ignoring the standards completely in favor of local control and inertia. The majority of these articles call for a moderate approach. As an example, science as an academic discipline is summarized as follows: The science standards are not a national science curriculum or a federal mandate. They do not contain specifications for a national exam. They are not a set of rules, regulations, or approaches.

Standards are designed to move stakeholders in the following directions:

- Teaching the discipline for conceptual change
- Promoting integration of the discipline and other content areas
- Placing students in positions for them to see themselves as potential professionals and critical thinkers using specific content
- Providing a foundation for teachers to create experiences promoting inquiry, wonder, and understanding

Overall, most of the literature calls for the various standards to provide a frame of reference for judging the quality of specific content education that is already provided. In addition, and most important, the standards should be used as a tool that can serve and inspire the teacher.

Classroom Applications

When structuring a semester or yearlong content experience for a class, there are only so many resources that can contribute to content and instructional practices. Some teachers turn to textbooks and their colleagues for concrete help in structuring day-to-day activities. They trust the textbook to cover the mandated content and colleagues to help provide the timeline or pace, choice of specific content, and related activities. Most of these choices are based on the resources available at the school and the department's institutionalized instructional inertia. It is crucial that teachers research and explore the various national frameworks, guidelines, and mandates. Specific guidelines, mandates, standards, and frameworks, provided by national content or curriculum organizations, filter through state and other bureaucratic agencies. Each state and district modifies and adapts these sources of guidance.

A quick search using various Internet search engines picked up too many "hits" to print. These sites feature a variety of content standards and guidelines in all content areas. Three valid and useful examples of national curriculum guidelines come from (1) the National Academy of Sciences, (2) the National Science Teachers Association, and (3) the American Association for the Advancement of Science (Project 2061). After reading many content standards in science over the years, it's clear the overall usefulness of these documents has improved. It is fair to assume other content areas are updating and becoming more valid and useful to teachers also. In the past, rarely would any of these documents filter down to the school site and classroom teacher. Today, because of access to the Internet, they are available to everyone. So now, rather than turning to the textbook or colleagues first, teachers may treat themselves to a more global perspective on how teaching and learning should be experienced by teachers and students alike.

In the recent past, the information in these documents was limited to what the authors of the guidelines thought should be taught. They have evolved their thinking and expanded their philosophy to present not only what should be taught but also how content should be taught, learned, and experienced by students. Most of them now include suggested content, delivery, and assessment strategies and standards. However, most don't give the teacher direct, concrete examples or activities ready for the classroom. They only suggest guidelines on how to create and construct a teacher's own experiences that are embedded in educational philosophy. If teachers are designing their own instructional strategies and activities, these types of documents are the best and most current sources of information available on a specific discipline. These articles can be interesting and motivating and should be visited and revisited in support of professional growth and inspiration.

Precautions and Possible Pitfalls

Not all teachers keep current on the latest ideas in teaching and learning. Department or school politics can be a problem. Curricular leadership can come into play and conflict. The standards, mandates, guidelines, and frameworks can be interpreted in different ways, and philosophical differences could also be problematic. There is no way to predict how change will affect the relationships within a given school or department.

Source

Bell, M., & Rakow, S. (1998). Science and young children: The message from the National Science Education Standards. *Childhood Education, 74*(3), 164-167.
DeCarlo, C. (1998). Standards that serve you. *Instructor, 108*(4), 71.

 Strategy 27: Use out-of-school learning environments. These unique learning opportunities can contribute to a more intrinsically motivating classroom environment.

What the Research Says

 Learning outside of school (informal education) plays a vital role in the development of competence in language, reading, mathematics, and a variety of other school-related domains.

Assume that such learning also contributes to classroom learning, motivation, and attitudes. Informal learning experiences help preschool children acquire a wide range of early literacy before the children enter school. They learn a language, usually before entering any formal classroom!

In this study, structured interviews of parents with elementary school children revealed the nature and scope of children's science-related activities outside of school. Research exposed a remarkable level of participation in extracurricular, science-related activities. Categories of participation included both nonfiction and science fiction television shows as well as reading activities, computer use, community activities such as zoos, home observations and simple science experiments, questioning and discussion, and household interest and familiarity with science. Often, time and interaction with science-related activities outside the formal science classroom exceeds time in the classroom.

While this study of informal learning looked primarily at science activities, it would come as no surprise to find the same sort of informal connections to the other disciplines.

Classroom Applications

The studies make it clear that learning outside of school should not be ignored and can be a new source of motivating instructional strategies. If science students are required to spend only a few hours a week in science instruction, the overall role schooling plays in developing science literacy is questionable. The influence of home and community environments needs to become a factor in planning more formalized content instruction.

Simple structured interviews or questionnaires can yield insights and characterize the development of content thinking from outside the school boundaries. This knowledge can yield a perspective on common experiences (e.g., exhibits at a museum) that can facilitate discussions, interpret phenomena, and frame classroom lessons and activities. Information could also serve to highlight a range of motivations and competencies among students and help teachers identify areas in which student "experts" could make a contribution to classroom learning, content projects, or other activities. It also can help identify influential allies at home who can reinforce your efforts with individual students or act as a broader class resource.

There is a full range of informal content-related activities students bring to your class. While this informal activity or exploration may diminish or change as students get older, much of their background and attitudes are based on this informal education. It may also become more specialized as a student finds some disciplines more interesting than others.

By remaining cognitive of the influence home and community environments have on overall content literacy; teachers can begin to incorporate the information into their instructional practices. Creative teachers can explore, enhance, and develop a range of curricular connections to the students' informal background.

Precautions and Possible Pitfalls

 School learning is often seen in a less enjoyable and sometimes more threatening light than the informal learning students encounter outside of the classroom. Much of the students' experience outside the classroom can be classified as *edutainment*. Integrating the two realms is a challenging but very do-able task. Research into the connections is just beginning to illuminate instructional relationships and doesn't yet offer a wide range of tested curricula to use the knowledge. Don't let the lack of formal connections discourage you! Create your own strategies to integrate the two paradigms within your instruction objectives and comfort zone.

Using resources outside the classroom can be a source of inequity due to access problems. Not all students have supportive parents or parents that can provide resources. If you're going to offer credit or ask students to visit or use resources outside of the classroom, offer a classroom or school-based option to those that can't participate off-campus.

Sources

Korpan, C. A., Bisanz, G. L., Bisanz, J., Boehme, C., & Lynch, M. A. (1997). What did you learn outside of school today? Using structured interviews to document home and community activities related to science and technology. *Science Education, 81*(6), 651-662.

Ramsey-Gassert, L. (1997). Learning science beyond the classroom. *Elementary School Journal, 97*(4), 433-450.

 Strategy 28: Use student peers to scaffold each other's learning.

What the Research Says

Peer tutoring can promote learning at virtually all grade and school levels. Research shows that peers can scaffold each other's development of higher-level thinking and learning.

One study of seventh graders learning science assigned students to three different tutoring conditions: explanation only, inquiry with explanation, and sequenced inquiry with explanation. Students were assigned to tutoring pairs and trained to tutor.

Tutoring occurred over five weeks on content the teacher had already covered. Researchers measured cognitive, metacognitive, and affective variables. The results showed that students do not have to be with other students who are more competent to develop their own thinking and knowledge. Students who are the same age and ability levels helped each other learn in all three conditions (King, Staffieri, & Adelgais, 1998).

A whole classroom of students helping other students has been found to be an efficient and effective method of enhancing achievement. Twenty teachers participated in a study of classwide peer tutoring with 40 classrooms in elementary and middle schools. Half of the schools implemented classwide peer tutoring programs and half did not. Both urban and suburban schools participated in the study and students came from diverse backgrounds, both culturally and linguistically. There were three different categories of students: average achievers, low achievers without learning disabilities, and low achievers with learning disabilities.

The peer tutoring programs were conducted three days a week, 35 minutes a day, for 15 weeks. Stronger students were paired with weaker students. Teachers reviewed each pair to ensure they were socially compatible. In all pairs, students took turns serving in the roles of tutor and tutee. Student pairs worked together for four weeks; then teachers arranged new pairings. Teachers received training on how to train their students to be tutors. Tutor training included teaching students how to correct each other's errors.

Achievement tests were administered before and after the peer-tutoring program. Regardless of whether students were average achievers or low achievers, with or without learning disabilities, students in the peer tutoring classrooms achieved at higher levels than those in the classrooms without classwide peer tutoring.

Classroom Applications

There are many areas in all disciplines that lend themselves to a peer-tutoring program. When there is a skill or skills to be learned and all one needs is experience with success or in understanding something covered by the teacher or text, then peer tutoring can provide an efficient way to monitor and support a student trying to master the skill or knowledge.

Disciplines other than math may have a full range of student math competencies within the same class. Say a student has difficulty with a math problem within an activity in a discipline other than math. If the student hasn't had geometry, others in the class might have and can act as tutors. Part of the student's problem is to recognize which calculation is called for and when more than one type of calculation may be used. It can get doubly confusing. Here a peer tutor (under the guidance of a teacher) can be quite beneficial. A student who has difficulty doing dilution factors or converting moles could find a peer tutor a genuine asset in a chemistry class. Additionally, the tutors in explaining these calculations to the students, are also provided with an opportunity to strengthen their own understanding of both the concept of the application (a higher-order thinking skill) and the role of math in science. Thus, there is often a mutual benefit to a peer-tutoring program.

Precautions and Possible Pitfalls

A tutor-training program offered by the teacher must precede peer tutoring. Tutors must be given some instruction on how to conduct the sessions, what sort of difficulties to look for on the part of the tutee and what points to stress in the sessions (based on the teacher's assessment of the class). Any individual difficulties on the part of the tutees should be mentioned to the tutor prior to the sessions. Tutors should be taught to guide student learning and not merely solve problems for students. Students with severe learning disabilities may pose a challenge to classwide peer tutoring, unless the tutors first receive individualized instruction from learning disabilities specialists.

Sources

Fuchs, D., Fuchs, L., Mathes, P. G., & Simmons, D. (1997). Peer-assisted learning strategies: Making classrooms more responsive to diversity. *American Educational Research Journal, 34*(1), 174-206.

King, A., Staffieri, A., & Adelgais, A. (1998). Mutual peer tutoring: Effects of structuring tutorial interaction to scaffold peer learning. *Journal of Educational Psychology, 90*(1), 134-152.

Strategy 29: Increase your understanding of personal learning styles. Try to improve the alignment between teacher and student awareness of learner preferences.

What the Research Says

Tobias (1986) characterized introductory college science courses by negative features such as failure to motivate student interest, passive learning, emphasis on competitive rather than cooperative learning, and reliance on algorithms rather than understanding. These features sometimes steer students away from careers in the sciences. Recent research suggests the mismatch between teaching practices and students' learning styles may account for many of these problems. Felder's (1993) model of learning styles is especially appealing because it conceptualizes the dimensions of sensing-intuiting, visual-verbal, inductive-deductive, active-reflective, and global-sequential as a continuum rather than as dichotomous either/or variables. Felder cites research to guide instruction for each of these styles.

Classroom Applications

Felder recommends the systematic use of a few additional teaching methods that overlap learning styles and contribute to the needs of all students. These include giving students experience with problems before giving them the tools to solve them, balancing concrete with conceptual information, liberally using graphic representations, physical analogies, and demonstrations, and showing students how concepts are connected within and between subjects and to everyday life experience.

Precautions and Possible Pitfalls

Students and parents often have an entrenched view of how a specific class is presented and will be experienced. If the teacher ventures too far from the norm, the students' comfort level can drop and their anxiety rises. If the teachers feel that they are presenting teaching or learning experiences (restructuring or reforming) that might be new or unfamiliar, they should consider clearly communicating these new strategies early. Teachers do not want to threaten students' potential success in their class or produce unneeded frustration.

Beware of the dangerous tendency to fall into the trap of labeling students, or allowing them to label themselves, as particular types of learners and restricting teaching and learning to the dominant styles. Ignoring nondominant styles can limit students' intellectual growth and development. The goal of thinking about students' learning styles is to facilitate learning—not constrain it.

Teachers shouldn't expect miracles of themselves. There can be an overwhelming number and variety of learning styles within a particular class, and it's unrealistic for teachers to regularly accommodate instruction to all of them. The key is to vary instructional methods and present information in multiple modalities.

Sources

Felder, R. (1993, March/April). Reaching the second tier: Learning and teaching styles in college science education. *Journal of College Science Teaching*, 23, 286-290.

Tobias, S. (1986, March-April). Peer perspectives on the teaching of science. *Change*, 36-41.

Strategy 30: Expand the range of opportunities rubrics offer. They can help teachers clarify their expectations for themselves and for their students.

What the Research Says

Research has found that teachers at various academic levels are exploring the use of rubrics in their classes. In this general survey, teacher at all levels used rubrics for assessment and for many other purposes within their instructional practices. Each application transforms the rubric to another purpose and the rubric can become a specialized instrument. Researchers investigating the use of rubrics in their own secondary methods courses found certain benefits and detriments in their use.

The benefits include reflective practice among students and instructors within the methods class and among the students using rubrics in their own classes. The detriments are related to issues of time and the clarity of the rubric's content. Researchers found that incorporating rubrics into instruction can benefit a course in two general areas. First, rubrics are tools that can be used to encourage reflective practice in both a temporal and a spatial sense. They model effective organizational strategies for students. Second, they are important in the development of professional knowledge through reflection and revisiting the rubric that is constructed. They force teachers to clarify the goals of the class and the goals of the specific lesson. Rubrics begin a discourse between students and teachers, and instruction, content, and assessment.

More specific detriments include a class "addiction" to rubrics in that they learn to depend on them. In addition, students and teachers find that once implemented, sometimes the rubric doesn't fit and needs modification; therefore, its validity suffers.

Researchers found that 75% of teachers who experienced rubrics in secondary science methods classes now used rubrics in their own classes. Overall, like concept maps and portfolios, rubrics, once mastered and practiced, prove to be a positive addition to the teacher's instructional toolbox.

Classroom Applications

Before a discussion about rubrics can begin, it is important to clarify the term. The National Science Education Standards (NRC, 1996) states a rubric is "a standard of performance for a defined population." Others have described rubrics as guidelines laid out for judging student work on performance-based tasks. Still others describe a rubric as an established set of criteria used for scoring or rating students' tests, portfolios, or performances.

Generally, rubrics must be able to answer the following questions:

1. What do we want students to know and be able to do with the instruction?

2. How well do we want students to know instructional information and related processes; what do we want them to do with the instructional information and processes?

3. How will the teachers and others know when the student masters the instruction and related processes or how well they master it?

There are no prescribed procedures for developing rubrics in science education. Constructs are very dependent upon the context of their use. A transfer of one rubric to another teacher and class simply would not work most of the time. Yet, examining rubrics from other classes is an important developmental activity and leads to professional growth.

One good suggestion for the construction of a rubric starts with writing performance standards. These can be found in many curriculum guides and frameworks. These standards should then be analyzed and divided into different components and complexity levels. The complexity and rigor of the rubric is then based on the experience and ability level of the students' and a teacher's goals.

Development of rubrics can come from three perspectives: holistic, analytical, or a combination of both. Holistic rubrics are instruments that contain different levels of performance that describe both the quantity and the quality of the task. The instructor determines the best fit for aspects of the lesson for the students. Analytical rubrics are constructs that consist of criteria that are further subdivided into different levels of performance. Start with criteria to be assessed and move on to different levels of performance for the criteria. Analytical rubrics tend to be more precise and concise while holistic rubrics contain broader descriptions about levels of performance.

Typing the word "rubric" into an Internet search engine can yield many good Web sites that can get a teacher started or can further refine and develop each personal rubric philosophy. Whichever style a teacher decides to synthesize, the rubric should try to involve students in patterns of observation, reflection, thinking, and problem solving that reflect the standards of the scientific community as reflected in various standards for content and scientific processes.

Precautions and Possible Pitfalls

Teachers should keep in mind that a major long-term goal of instruction is to have students be able to decide, on their own, what they need to know, how they need to know it, and when they need to know it. Rubrics can create dependence and do not foster "learning how to learn" strategies unless teachers deliberately build this goal into their strategies to reduce the students' dependence on them.

At some point, the teacher should collaborate with the students in the development of mutually agreed-upon rubrics. The exercise becomes guided practice in transferring some responsibility to the students for their own learning.

Sources

Luft, J. A. (1999). Rubrics: Design and use in science teacher education. *Journal of Science Teacher Education, 10*(2), 107-121.

National Research Council. (1996). *National education standards*. Washington, DC: National Academy Press. Retrieved July 2002 from bob.nap.edu/readingroom/books/nses/html/5.html#dsdl.

Strategy 31: Establish scaffolds for complex skills and procedures. Temporary support (scaffolds) helps students as they are learning complex skills or procedures.

What the Research Says

Walberg (1991) suggests that in science it is especially useful for students to struggle with interesting, meaningful problems that can stimulate discussion about competing approaches. This idea can be stretched to include all disciplines. He recommends using what he calls *comprehension teaching*, more commonly called *scaffolding*, which involves providing students with temporary support until they can perform tasks on their own. Based on Vygotsky's (1978) concept of the "zone of proximal development," scaffolding is recommended for teachers to build from what students can do only with temporary guidance from a more competent person, gradually reducing and eventually removing this support as students become independent thinkers and learners who can perform the task or use the skill on their own. The zone of proximal development refers to the area within which the student can receive support from another to successfully perform a task until able to perform it independently. Scaffolding has been found to be an excellent method of developing students' higher-level thinking skills (Rosenshine & Meiester, 1992). Scaffolding is a strategy for gradually and systematically shifting responsibility and control over learning and performance from the teacher to the student.

Classroom Applications

Through a variety of methods (e.g., observation, listening, tests), assess students' abilities to perform and not perform important skills or tasks independently. Test their ability to perform or not perform these skills or tasks with assistance from another, in order to conceptualize their zone of proximal development. Teachers can use a scaffolding approach for skills and tasks that are within the students' zone. Scaffolds can range from a simple hint, clue, example, or question to a complex sequence of activities that begin with teacher-centered approaches (e.g., explaining, demonstrating) but end as student-centered (e.g., self-questioning, self-monitoring).

The example that follows is a scaffolding approach to teaching students to construct graphic organizers of text they have read. It is a complex sequence of steps that uses scaffolding to shift from teacher direction and control of creating graphic organizers to student self-direction and self-control over making them.

1. Show and explain a variety of traditional examples of graphic organizers, such as flow charts, concept maps, and matrices, made by both professionals and students.

2. Inform students about what graphic organizers are and when, why, and how to use various types of them. One source (Jones, Pierce, & Hunter, 1988/1989) provides information on why and how to create graphic organizers to comprehend text. It provides illustrations of a spider map, a continuum or scale, a series of events chain, a compare-contrast matrix, a problem-solution outline, a network tree, a fishbone map, a human interaction outline, and a cycle. Another source focuses on concept maps and Vee diagrams (Novak, 1998).

3. As classwork or a homework assignment, give students a partially completed graphic organizer to finish on their own. Give students feedback on their completions.

4. Assign classwork or homework that requires students to complete an empty graphic organizer structure entirely on their own. Give students feedback.

5.   Assign classwork or homework requiring groups of students to create their own graphic organizers. Give students specific criteria or rubrics for constructing and evaluating graphic organizers. Sample criteria include (a) neat and easy to read, (b) ideas are expressed clearly, (c) ideas are expressed completely but succinctly, (d) content is organized clearly and logically, (e) labels or other strategies (colors, lines) are used to guide the reader's comprehension, (f) main ideas, not minor details, are emphasized, (g) it is visually appealing, and (h) the reader doesn't have to turn the page to read the words.

6.   Once their graphic organizers are completed, the individual groups show their graphic organizers to the other groups, which critique the graphic organizers and give them feedback based on the criteria identified above. Teachers should supplement the feedback as needed.

7.   For homework, students develop graphic organizers completely on their own, using the identified criteria. Group members give each other homework feedback on the extent to which they met the established criteria.

8.   Finally, students are expected to be able to create and critique their own graphic organizers, and support from others (students and professor) isn't needed.

Precautions and Possible Pitfalls

To use scaffolding effectively it is vital for teachers to consider issues such as what types of support to provide and when and what order to sequence them in, and to figure out the criteria for deciding when it is time to reduce or withdraw support from students. It is also very important to make sure scaffolding attempts are truly within the students' zone of proximal development. If they are below this area, activities will be too easy because the student can really do them independently. If they are above this area, no amount of scaffolding will enable students to perform independently because the skill or task is too difficult given the students' prior knowledge or skills.

Sources

Jones, B. F., Pierce, J., & Hunter, B. (1988/1989). Teaching students to construct graphic representations. *Educational Leadership, 46*(4), 20-25.

Novak, J. (1998). *Learning, creating and using knowledge: Concept maps as facilitative tools in schools and corporations.* Mahwah, NJ: Erlbaum.

Rosenshine, B., & Meiester, C. (1992). The use of scaffolds for teaching higher-level cognitive strategies. *Educational Leadership, 49*(7), 26-33.

Vygotsky, L. S. (1978). *Mind in society: The development of higher psychological processes.* Cambridge, MA: Harvard University Press.

Walberg, H. (1991). Improving school science in advanced and developing countries. *Review of Educational Research, 61*(1), 25-69.

Strategy 32: Create new strategies to encourage more student questions.

What the Research Says

Several approaches have been identified that can help to overcome students' reluctance to ask questions:

1. Avoid giving students the impression that the reasons for difficulties are their own.

2. In cases where students have difficulties with problems, do not indicate that the problem was simple.

3. Give external reasons for students' difficulties.

Research has shown that people can handle their neediness better if they can attribute the reasons for their neediness to external causes. One study investigated asking questions as a kind of neediness. Participants were 24 girls and 24 boys, with a mean age of 14 years. Students were confronted with the following situation. They were given an unformatted text that included typing mistakes. Students had to format the text according to a given pattern. The results showed

1. Students showed the most willingness to ask questions when they could hold external circumstances responsible for their neediness.

2. Students' willingness to ask questions decreased when they had the impression that the person they asked blamed them for the difficulty. In this case, if the students asked questions it would hurt their self-esteem.

3. Students avoided asking questions if the person they asked indicated the task was simple.

Classroom Applications

Teachers should explicitly and implicitly encourage students to ask questions. Asking questions is not easy for students in many cases. Sometimes even simple questions require both a minimum of knowledge or understanding and courage. Teachers should help students feel that there are no such things as silly questions, although teachers sometimes give silly answers! Asking questions is one of the most valuable skills a person can develop. Teachers can say that silly questions are often the very best questions. Teachers should give positive comments about students' questions. Examples include

- "Good question!"
- "Instead of getting grades for good answers, you should get grades for good questions!"
- "Your questions show that you've thought about this a lot."
- "Very interesting question!"

Encourage students to ask questions by emphasizing the difficulties of the task or of the working conditions. Assume the role of an active educational coworker with your students. For example,

- "Some aspects of this problem are hidden. Consequently, even the teacher might have some difficulties."
- "We never even talked about some of the steps needed to solve this problem."
- "Tomorrow we'll review how to solve that type of problem. Lots of students seem to be confused, so get your questions ready."
- "I didn't even see this problem."
- "Even today I have to struggle when asking questions in public."

If students begin to attribute difficulties to their own lack of ability, try to direct their attention to the external difficulties. Examples include

- "Make sure you pay careful attention to the difficult parts of this problem."
- "This is a new type of problem. We haven't discussed it yet, so you're not expected to know how to solve it right now."
- "Do not expect your brain to work very quickly. It has been a long day."

Do not express doubt or make negative remarks about students' capabilities or skills. Examples include

- "I already answered that question three times."
- "Listen carefully to what I say!"

Use more thoughtful replies, such as

- "When students ask me a question a third time, that tells me that something has gone wrong with my explanation."

- "Okay! We covered a lot of facts—maybe too much."
- "Sometimes I explain things too quickly."

Have groups of students answer each other's questions and any questions they can't answer can be submitted to the teacher as the group's questions, thereby saving face for the individual student.

Precautions and Possible Pitfalls

Beware of a possible strategy backfire! When explaining an assignment's difficulties from external circumstances (very abstract, complex, obscure or obtuse, pressured for time, or application of a rarely used technique, etc.) you might encourage and motivate students. However, the teacher can also confirm or support the student's opinion that the assignment is too difficult anyway. In that case students would not be encouraged, but would feel justified in stopping working on the problem and questioning will cease!

Source

Fuhrer, U. (1994). Fragehemmungen bei Schulerinnen und Schulern: Eine attributierungstheoretische Erklärung [Pupils' inhibition to ask questions: An attributional analysis]. *Zeitschrift fur Pädagogische Psychologie, 8,* 103-109.

Strategy 33: Fit it all in by making realistic time estimates during lesson planning.

What the Research Says

Teachers need to have excellent time-management skills for students to learn effectively. It is sometimes said that "time + energy = learning." Sometimes there's confusion between the time teachers allocate for instruction, e.g., a 50-minute class period, and the time students are actually engaged in learning, which may only be 25 minutes out of the 50 allocated. The concept of engaged time is often referred to as "time-on-task." Teachers often fail to take into account the off-task time they devote to managing student behavior, managing classroom activities, and dealing with announcements and interruptions.

Classroom Applications

 Distinguish between time allocated for instruction and engaged learning time when estimating how much time it will take for students to learn a particular set of material. It's the time students actually spend learning that is the key to the amount of achievement.

Precautions and Possible Pitfalls

Teachers need to be sure to plan time in their lessons for students to digest the material covered, to monitor their comprehension of concepts and tasks, and to engage in clarification as needed. Looking at a lesson only from a teacher's point of view of making sure material is taught or covered, the teacher is likely to underestimate the time students need to understand, record, and remember what they have learned. Teachers should make sure to allow sufficient note-taking time to help to ensure that students have time to take complete notes of the development being done in the lesson, so that they can effectively review for tests at home.

Source

Brophy, J. (1988). Research linking teacher behavior to student achievement: Potential implications for instruction of Chapter 1 students. *Educational Psychologist, 23,* 235-286.

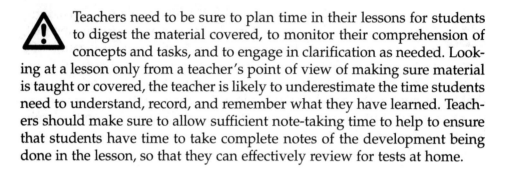

Strategy 34: Create more stimulating and successful questioning techniques.

What the Research Says

There is evidence that much of teaching amounts to "telling," which students find boring. Research suggests that when teachers do ask questions, most of them are at a relatively low level. When teachers ask a majority of low-level questions (e.g., identify, define, describe) student achievement does not reach levels as high as when students are asked mostly higher-level questions (e.g., predict, justify, evaluate) (Redfield & Rousseau, 1981).

Research was conducted to investigate what questions teachers asked and why they asked them. Thirty-six high school teachers from five schools, representing all subject areas, participated in the study. They were asked to give examples of the questions they asked, to explain how they used them, and to tell to whom the questions were addressed. These results along with findings from previous research by Bloom, Engelhart, Furst, Hill, and Krathwohl (1956), Tisher (1971), and Smith and Meux (1970) led to a system of classifying types of questions teachers ask in the classroom.

Classroom Applications

There are many types of questions to use as well as many to avoid. Learning science requires understanding. When a topic that requires thought and deduction is being considered, it is usually helpful to ask lots of questions. Questions should be formulated with respect to long-term learning goals and should be succinctly structured to guide students' development so they can think like scientists. Questions can range from those which require low-level responses (e.g., recalling facts for definitions and descriptions), to those requiring intermediate-level responses (e.g., classifying and comparing or contrasting), to those requiring high-level responses (e.g., predicting, evaluating), which may have no definite answer, but require a judgment to be made. The following is the classified system mentioned above of types of questions teachers ask in the classroom.

Cognitive Questions

1. *Recalling data, task procedures, values, or knowledge.* This category includes naming, classifying, reading out loud, providing known definitions, and observing. These are low-level questions. For example, "How many stages are there in meiosis?"

2. *Making simple deductions usually based on data that have been provided.* This category includes comparing, giving simple descriptions and interpretations, and giving examples of principles. These are intermediate-level questions. For example, "How does the Vietnam conflict compare with World War II?"

3. *Giving reasons, hypotheses, causes, or motives that were not taught in the lesson.* These are high-level questions. For example, "What are possible explanations of the latest stock market decline that are not in our book?"

4. *Solving problems, using sequences of reasoning.* These are high-level questions. For examples, "What steps would you take to solve that problem? What order do they go in?"

5. *Evaluating one's own work, a topic, or a set of values.* These are high-level questions. For example, "Did I make any careless mistakes? How can I verify my answer?"

Speculative, Affective, and Management Questions

1. *Making speculations, intuitive guesses, creative ideas or approaches, and open-ended questions (which have more than one right answer and permit a wide range of responses).* For example, "Approximately how long will it take before the chemical reaction we're expecting takes place? How do you think we'll know if it worked? How else could we produce that reaction?"

2. *Encouraging expressions of empathy and feelings.* For example, "How do you think she felt when her ceramic art project was dropped?"

3. *Managing individuals, groups, or the entire class.* This category includes checking that students understand a task, seeking compliance, controlling a situation, and directing students' attention. For example, "Which groups solved the problem? Which groups need help?"

There are many different questioning taxonomies teachers can consult to help them vary the types and levels of questions they ask. Sigel, McGuillicudy-DeLisi, and Johnson's taxonomy (1980) has three levels: low (e.g., identify, describe) intermediate, and high. Teachers should spend most of their time questioning at intermediate and high levels.

Intermediate-Order Questions

Intermediate-order questions require the answerer to

- Describe or infer similarities
- Sequence
- Describe or infer differences
- Analyze
- Apply
- Classify
- Estimate
- Synthesize

Higher-Order Questions

Higher-order questions require the answerer to

- Evaluate
- Verify
- Infer causal relations
- Conclude
- Propose alternatives
- Predict outcomes
- Resolve conflicts

- Generalize
- Transform
- Plan

Precautions and Possible Pitfalls

Even good questions can lose their value if they are overused. Avoid asking ambiguous questions and questions requiring only one-word answers such as yes-no questions. Focusing on a questioning style as indicated above, but without proper concern to the subject matter, would be a misuse of this strategy.

Sources

Bloom, B. S., Engelhart, M. D., Furst, E. J., Hill, W. H., & Krathwohl, D. R. (1956). *Taxonomy of educational objectives: The classification of educational goals.* New York: David McKay.

Brown, G. A., & Edmondson, R. (1984). Asking questions. In E. C. Wragg (Ed.), *Classroom teaching skills.* New York: Nichols.

Redfield, D., & Rousseau, E. (1981). A meta-analysis of experimental research on teacher questioning behavior. *Review of Educational Research, 51*(2), 237-245.

Sigel, I. E., McGuillicudy-DeLisi, A. V., & Johnson, J. E. (1980). *Parental distancing beliefs and children's representational competence within the family context.* Princeton, NJ: Educational Testing Service.

Smith, B., & Meux, M. (1970). *A study of the logic of teachings.* Chicago: University of Illinois Press.

Tisher, R. P. (1971). Verbal interaction in science classes. *Journal of Research in Science Teaching, 8,* 1-8.

 ### Strategy 35: Make the most of one-on-one student contacts.

What the Research Says

Frequent contact between teachers and students helps students develop academically and intellectually. Rich teacher-student interaction creates a stimulating environment, encourages students to explore ideas and approaches, and allows teachers to guide or mentor individual students according to their individual needs.

Classroom Applications

Working with individual students in a traditional classroom setting is not practical for long periods of time. While students are working individually on an exercise, the teacher should visit with individual students and offer them some meaningful suggestions. Such suggestions might include hints on moving a student who appears frustrated or bogged down on a point toward a solution.

These private comments to students might also be in the form of advice regarding the form of the student's work. That is, some students are their own worst enemy when they are doing a geometry problem and working with a diagram which is either so small that they cannot do anything worthwhile with it or so inaccurately drawn that it, too, proves to be relatively useless. Such small support offerings will move students along and give them that very important feeling of teacher interest.

In some cases, when a student experiences more severe problems, the teacher might be wise to work with individual students after classroom hours. In the latter situation, it would be advisable to have the student describe the work as it is being done, trying to justify the procedures and explain concepts. During such one-on-one tutoring sessions, the teacher can get a good insight into the student's problems. Are they conceptual? Has the student missed understanding an algorithm? Does the student have perceptual difficulties or spatial difficulties? And so on.

Precautions and Possible Pitfalls

To work with individual students and merely make perfunctory comments, when more might be expected, could be useless when considering that the severity of a possible problem might warrant more attention. Teachers should make every effort to give proper attention to students when attempting to react to this teaching strategy. Teachers should keep the student's level in mind so that, where appropriate, they can add some spice to the individual sessions by providing a carefully selected range and choice of challenges to the student so that there may be a further individualization in the learning process. Teachers should make sure good students don't get bored. Challenge them by giving them more difficult problems to solve, having them tutor other students, or having them evaluate alternative approaches to solving a problem.

Be aware that some students can become very needy. They often lack confidence or the ability to work comfortably in an independent manner. This can compel them to begin to dominate your time. When this occurs, give them the same general attention that you give to others. When their demands begin to dominate the class, invite them to see you after school or at a time when you can give them undivided attention. To conserve time, consider combining a few students with the same problems and address their needs together. Or, have students who understand the material serve as tutors, mentors, or group leaders.

Source

Pressley, M., & McCormick, C. (1995). *Advanced educational psychology*. New York: HarperCollins.

Strategy 36: Fight boredom by using class-room strategies that stimulate student interest. Varying instructional strategies can stimulate student interest.

What the Research Says

 A study following high school students for three years found that a relationship exists between students' interests and investments in their work at school and their teachers' reper-toire of techniques for engaging them (Wasley, Hampel, & Clark, 1997).

Classroom Applications

Although each new school year brings about enthusiasm and opti-mism for students and teachers, once students encounter instruc-tional routines and procedures that become predictable, their enthusiasm for learning may begin to wane.

By using a range of instructional strategies from one unit to the next, student interest is stimulated. For example, a teacher might have students listen to a speech, discuss it in a group, and then write a paper about the speech. Following this project the teacher may have students do a group assignment about favorite speeches and the people who gave them. Students could finish up this unit by either delivering their favorite speech or writing one of their own. The instructional model of reading the book, answering the questions at the end of the chapter, listening to a lecture or watching a video, and taking a test does not provide for good instruction. There is no research to support that this method is effective.

Essential to the success of varying instructional strategies is support from school districts in providing professional growth opportunities for teachers by encouraging them to attend workshops or seminars or to network with colleagues about best teaching practices. Also of critical importance is the reflection by the teacher after a lesson is taught. Another powerful strategy is to invite observation by fellow colleagues or mentors. An observation of a novice teacher's lesson and the reflective conversation afterward can be a "mirror" to the novice of what is really going on in the classroom. These mentors can help novice teachers understand that mirroring is essential to their development as professionals.

In many teacher induction programs around the country, districts are now focusing on helping new teachers build a repertoire of techniques, skills, and strategies through ongoing professional development. Districts must allow time for new teachers to attend seminars, conferences, and observations of exemplary teachers to assist these emerging teachers in building a repertoire that is responsive to the students they serve.

Precautions and Possible Pitfalls

Teachers sometimes fall into a pattern of using a particular strategy (especially if it has been successful) to the detriment of using any others. Although it is important for new teachers to take risks in the classroom, it is just as important to learn what works and what doesn't in a particular classroom setting. Students like consistency and routine to a point; however, if the instructional strategies are never varied, the students become bored and disinterested. Do not be afraid to consult with a veteran teacher on ways to vary strategies, whether it is on the type of assessment being used or using Socratic dialogue to generate student opinions on a piece of literature. It is important to remember that no one technique or strategy works every time with every student.

Source

Wasley, P., Hampel, R., & Clark, R. (1997). *Kids and school reform.* San Francisco: Jossey-Bass.

Strategy 37: Master the art of questioning by building in wait time.

What the Research Says

There is an art to questioning and one that is frequently overlooked by novice teachers. While teachers spend time planning lessons, designing assessment, and grading homework, little thought is given to the importance of using questioning in a student-centered classroom. Of particular importance, but often neglected, is the concept of "wait time."

Wait time may be defined as the time a teacher waits after asking a question before talking again (Rowe, 1986). Too often a teacher asks a question and then expects an immediate response. Research shows that the longer the pause (three to five seconds), the more thoughtful the response. The use of wait time is especially useful when asking higher-order questions. A study of preservice teachers who observed middle and high school science classes on the East Coast reported that with little or no wait time, short answers were elicited. When the wait time was increased, the caliber of answers was greater (Freedman, 2000). In this same study, teachers reported that on a typical day they asked about 24 questions in a 40-minute class period. The number of convergent questions was twice that of divergent ones, and they asked the same percentage of lower-order questions (knowledge and comprehension) as higher-order questions (application, analysis, synthesis, and evaluation). When asked what they could do to expand into more desirable questioners, their answer was "more planning."

Classroom Applications

 Teachers need to plan and practice the types of questions they will be asking their students. Questioning can be used for many purposes, including checking for understanding, determining students' prior knowledge, beginning a class discussion, or stimulating critical thinking. Questions should be part of the lesson planning process and should be planned just as other parts of the lesson are. The simple counting to self (one-thousand one, one-thousand two, . . .) can help remind teachers to wait after asking a question.

Using a mentor or colleague can help a teacher evaluate and improve his or her questioning practice. Having the observer write down the questions asked, while the lesson is being taught, and then reflecting back on that lesson can be useful in assisting new teachers in the improvement of their practice. Another excellent method for reflection is to videotape the teacher while teaching a lesson. The teacher can then see how questions were asked, if they were convergent or divergent, and the amount of wait time that was allowed. All these factors can help novices learn their craft.

Precautions and Possible Pitfalls

Be careful not to get caught up in always asking the same type of questions, asking the same students, and expecting a correct answer each time. When asking a question of a specific student, it is important that other students do not shout out the answer if the designated student doesn't answer immediately. Sometimes it is better to ask the question first, then call on a student. This will help reduce student passivity. In addition, if the teacher asks questions that invite reflection, the learning comes about as a result of a partnership between teacher and student.

Sources

Freedman, R. L. H. (2000). [Questioning strategies in Western New York teachers' science classrooms]. Unpublished raw data.

Rowe, N. B. (1986). Wait-time: Slowing down may be a way of speeding up. *Journal of Teacher Education, 37*(1), 43-50.

5

Using Student Assessment and Feedback to Maximize Instructional Effectiveness

 Strategy 38: Learn when to de-emphasize grades in your course or subject.

What the Research Says

Giving grades early in the learning process stimulates students to participate actively in their lessons, but may undermine achievement in the long run. Previous research provided evidence that students learn because of anxiety over grades or because they get good grades with a minimum of effort. Giving grades early is especially beneficial for students who require more time to understand things. They tend to be afraid of saying something wrong and of getting bad grades. Early grading is not viewed as judgmental about a student's knowledge. It is viewed more as informative than as judgmental.

This study investigated four ninth-grade classes on the effects of giving grades at an early stage of knowledge acquisition. To show the effects of early marking, four classes were separated into two groups. Both groups received computer-aided instruction and got a grade after every step. The first group did not get to know about their grades, while the second group was informed about their grades. The achievements of the groups were compared on the basis of the grade after every step and on a final test. Students who knew their marks did slightly better on the interim tests. Their learning was enhanced by the grades. In contrast, on the final test, students who did not know their interim grades did noticeably better. They were not pushed by pressure of marks. They used additional work to develop self-control. In this way, they dealt with the issue of their learning needs, they understood it profoundly, and they achieved at higher levels.

Classroom Applications

Teachers should avoid giving grades at an early stage of learning. Early marks can easily frustrate students who are not interested in a particular topic or even the whole subject and their motivation can sink even further. Although early grades can promote rapid success, in some cases this leads to students resting on their laurels. During the period students are acquiring new knowledge, the teacher should use grades sparingly.

Teachers need to remember that not all feedback needs to be evaluated with a grade. The process of learning and putting together a product is increasingly seen as more important than the finished product itself. Simply checking off a step or stamping work as completed before moving on to the next could be enough incentive (with feedback) to keep instruction (and learning) moving.

Precautions and Possible Pitfalls

The teacher should not stop all assessment during the early stage of learning. First, students need assessment to evaluate or at least estimate their own achievement. In addition, the teacher will always find some students who are entirely motivated by grades. Therefore, during the early learning phase, a teacher should use oral or nonverbal assessment techniques.

Source

Lechner, H. J., Brehm, R.-I., & Zbigniew, M. (1996). Zensierung und ihr Einfluß auf die Leistung der Schüler [Influence of marks on student achievement]. *Pädagogik und Schulalltag*, 51(3), 371-379.

Strategy 39: Reward students for paying attention to the feedback they're given.

What the Research Says

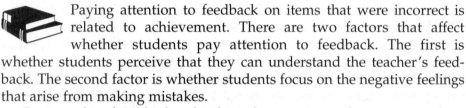

Paying attention to feedback on items that were incorrect is related to achievement. There are two factors that affect whether students pay attention to feedback. The first is whether students perceive that they can understand the teacher's feedback. The second factor is whether students focus on the negative feelings that arise from making mistakes.

In a study of 38 high school students in two classes, researchers observed how students processed feedback during computer programming lessons while the teacher discussed the results of a recent test. Observations were categorized into 10 on-task behaviors (e.g., looking at the teacher or writing on the test) and nine off-task behaviors (e.g., looking out the window or writing on irrelevant material).

Thirteen low- and high-achieving students were randomly selected for interviews to get more detailed information on how they processed feedback. One distinct pattern that frequently emerged was students' judgment that they could not understand the teacher's feedback. When students do understand the feedback, they listen to what the teacher is saying and try to figure out what they did wrong. When they do not understand the teacher's feedback, they tune out. The other pattern that emerged, but was less common, was getting upset about making errors. When this occurred, instead of focusing on the problem, students tended to focus on their negative feelings.

Classroom Applications

The teacher should try giving students an option of two due dates for an assignment. If they finish an assignment and turn it in for feedback on the first date, guarantee them a certain number of points or grade. Then, if they sincerely incorporate the teacher's feedback, they should be rewarded with a higher grade.

For the others, evaluation should be in a more traditional way after the second due date. While using this strategy in an academic science class, it is common to have 50% of the students take advantage of the first due date.

In another, related strategy, the teacher should evaluate students' work once and give them feedback, with no grade. A grade should be given only if they integrate the feedback suggestions into the assignment. Whether a teacher uses these strategies or modifies or makes up another, the teacher will begin to feel the feedback has real value to the students!

Precautions and Possible Pitfalls

Teachers should be aware of the fact that some of their comments, whether given individually or to the class, may be ignored or simply forgotten. Simple awareness of the importance of the students' retaining teacher feedback is already one big step in making this aspect of the instructional program effective. Journal entries or written error analyses can become tedious and should take on various forms. For example, the student might see this additional written assignment as a form of punishment.

If a teacher senses this, there should be an alternative way of reaching the same objective. In this case, the teacher may have a student who understood the teacher's feedback explain the problem and the teacher's resolution to a classmate.

Source

Gagne, E. D., Crutcher, R. J., Anzelc, J., Geisman, C., Hoffman, V., Schutz, P., & Lizcano, L. (1987). The role of student processing of feedback in classroom achievement. *Cognition and Instruction, 4*(3), 167–186.

 Strategy 40: Be prompt in giving students feedback about their performance.

What the Research Says

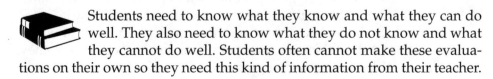 Students need to know what they know and what they can do well. They also need to know what they do not know and what they cannot do well. Students often cannot make these evaluations on their own so they need this kind of information from their teacher.

Information about their knowledge and performance, which is known as feedback, can help students focus their learning efforts and activities. This helps students learn. Feedback is more meaningful and more useful when delivered in a timely fashion.

Classroom Applications

In an inquiry or hands-on science classroom, teachers should ask students to set their homework out while they continue with an activity. The teacher can buy a few interesting rubber stamps to stamp completed or successful work and circle the room checking homework during the hands-on activity.

The teacher can look over the homework while guiding and supporting the ongoing hands-on activity. The teacher doesn't have to correct it and has the chance to give each student instant verbal feedback! The work can then become part of the students' notebooks. This way the teacher's prep period or at-home time can be saved for grading work that requires more attention.

Teachers need to keep in mind that it is very tempting to spot-check homework by inspecting to see if the right answers are offered without looking at the method to reach the answer. Whenever possible, teachers should thoroughly examine students' homework answers and methods; they should give students information about the quality of their performance. With practice, teachers will learn to recognize problems with the assignment faster and more easily. Within a class, it is common to find that the same problems pop up as problematic for a number of students.

Where a teacher's class is too large to do a thorough check of the homework, the teacher can select different subgroups from within the class daily, picking their homework from the collected class set.

Precautions and Possible Pitfalls

The teacher may either randomly select subgroups or select them by design. In any case, this selection should not be predictable by the students. Otherwise, those who anticipate homework inspection will do a better job. If feedback is not provided in a timely fashion, it will be of limited use to students.

Focusing on an assignment with the teacher's undivided attention can be difficult for some within a noisy and active class. It takes practice to become effective. The assessment and feedback must be authentic and not just rubber-stamped as completed or you run a risk of devaluing the students' effort and work.

Source

Chickering, A. W., & Gamson, Z. F. (1987). Seven principles for good practice in undergraduate education. *Wingspread Journal, 9*(2), special insert.

Strategy 41: *Improve student performance with well-crafted and precise teacher feedback.*

What the Research Says

Studies have shown that improved student performance results from the amount of feedback given to students. Students need to receive specific and personal feedback on the results of their practice in order for learning to be effective. Practice with specific feedback results in more successful and more efficient learning.

Classroom Applications

Within instructional practices in most disciplines, there are usually many opportunities to practice the skills presented. By pairing students and having them read each other's work, or by having students compare their work to model solutions, a form of feedback can be obtained regularly without a great expense of time. Teachers might also systematically review a small and different sampling of student papers each day and from this small number of collected papers provide some meaningful feedback to the students. For example, suppose that a classroom is situated in rows of students. The teacher may randomly call for papers from everyone sitting in the first seat of each row, from the students sitting on the diagonal, or from everyone in the third row. If a teacher wants to check on a particular student's paper a second day, as there may be some serious questions about the student's work, then the teacher can ask for the student's paper by including him or her in the second day's set of collected papers.

This can be achieved by calling on a second group that also corresponds to the particular student's seat, such as the third row one day and then, since the target student is sitting in the last seat of the row, a call for the papers from all students sitting in the last seat of a row the second day. This would inconspicuously include the target student a second time.

Since it is unreasonable to expect the teacher to do a thorough reading of everyone's paper every day, there are alternative ways to provide feedback to students on their homework. One could search for parent volunteers or retired teachers who might like to take on some part-time work in reading and reacting (in writing) to student work. One might also try to engage some older and more advanced students to undertake a similar activity, using a cross-age tutoring approach. This would also serve them well as they can benefit by looking back over previously learned material from a more advanced standpoint. By doing this, not only are the target students being helped, but the older students are deepening their knowledge of the discipline, theme, or process.

Precautions and Possible Pitfalls

 Teachers oftentimes do not have sufficient resources to provide individual feedback to each student. When having students give each other feedback, teachers should be aware that the feedback from students is of a different nature and certainly not a replacement for that provided by the teacher. Student feedback must be monitored to avoid perpetuating flawed ideas or misconceptions. The same holds true for teachers' aides, parent volunteers, or retirees assisting in the classroom.

Source

Benjamin, L. T., & Lowman, K. D. (Eds.). (1981). *Activities handbook for the teaching of psychology.* Washington, DC: American Psychological Association.

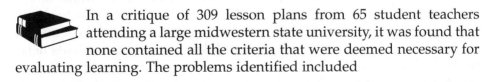

Strategy 42: Interface assessment strategies to instructional goals for powerful learning.

What the Research Says

In a critique of 309 lesson plans from 65 student teachers attending a large midwestern state university, it was found that none contained all the criteria that were deemed necessary for evaluating learning. The problems identified included

- An absence of a direct link between instructional goals and assessment
- Twenty-three percent featured nonobservable objectives, although the majority recognized the need
- Samples of 103 assessments where only eight assessment strategies were deemed complete

- The absence of reliability and validity concepts
- A huge discrepancy between measurement instruction from their university classes and its practical application among student teachers

Classroom Applications

During the history of public education there has never been a better time in which to find help on assessment and instructional practices. Today's course content has never been more analyzed by state framework writers, educational agencies, special interest groups, and parent organizations. The best of them feature not only content outlines but pedagogical and assessment suggestions and guidelines. In addition, most textbook publishers (who design their books based on the same documents) provide instruction and assessment strategies connected to their books' content.

Most subjects' content frameworks are now accessible via the Internet, and a master or supervising teacher can access the content textbook's support material. In addition, many veteran teachers use assessment strategies that connect to skills required on standardized tests. Teachers should analyze and use them all within their personal instructional contexts. It's clear the resources are there. The dilemma for new teachers is deciding which to use. Some of these resources offer more valid and reliable information, and the trick is finding a secure bridge between instructional goals, classroom instruction, and assessment. Also, all new teachers come with their own ideas about assessment or they adopt their master teachers' goals. Some framework and supplemental textbook information seems written by people who have never been in a classroom. Some others will stand out and seem to have been written just for the new teachers with their goals in mind. As a beginning teacher, you should survey as much information as you can access before synthesizing your own strategies.

The trick for new teachers is to construct the unit or lesson in a complete package with equal attention to goals and objectives, instructional delivery systems, and fair, reliable, and valid assessment strategies. If assessment is considered and addressed before beginning instruction, teachers will find peace of mind and security as they move the students toward final assessment. The teacher will know what the students need to be successful as the lesson progresses and will always have that in mind. In this way the teacher can always make adjustments to instruction and shorten or lengthen the pace, simplify or rework instructional trouble spots, or tweak the assessment a bit if necessary. There is a saying that if you don't know where you are going, you will probably never get there. With assessment, teachers should take it to heart; their students will thankthem and they will feel much more confident as a teacher.

Precautions and Possible Pitfalls

 For a new teacher, politics plays a heavy role in assessment. New teachers often find themselves split between using their master teachers' assessment instruments and strategies and developing their own. A solution to this dilemma is to codevelop the lesson or unit, including assessment, with the supervising teacher. Teachers should develop a resource bank of frameworks and other guidelines of their own and bring them to the table with them to support their ideas and their practices.

Also, students are often quick to blame the teacher for their lack of success on the assessment. The teacher needs to be prepared for these arguments. This is where veteran teachers can offer suggestions and help the beginning teachers as they prepare strategies for such situations, as they are better able to provide strategies due to their experience.

Source

Campbell, C., & Evans, J. A. (2000). Investigation of preservice teachers' classroom assessment practices during student teaching. *Journal of Educational Research, 93*(6), 350.

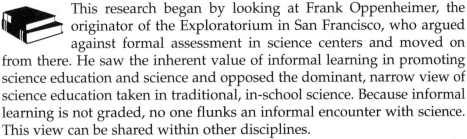

Strategy 43: Remember to consider alternate assessment styles and instruments.

What the Research Says

This research began by looking at Frank Oppenheimer, the originator of the Exploratorium in San Francisco, who argued against formal assessment in science centers and moved on from there. He saw the inherent value of informal learning in promoting science education and science and opposed the dominant, narrow view of science education taken in traditional, in-school science. Because informal learning is not graded, no one flunks an informal encounter with science. This view can be shared within other disciplines.

Some researchers believe that many informal experiences are so individual and multifaceted that they cannot be assessed with letter grades or scores. Some see the lack of evaluation as an obvious strength in engaging individuals in a more social, open-ended, learner-directed experience, with a less planned and nonevaluative contact with science. Trying to evaluate so many potential unintended outcomes is just not fair to students.

Out of four research papers that examined out-of-school informal educational activities, all used students' written reflections (some used a rubric to guide students' responses) to survey the students' perception of how much they learned and its quality.

Classroom Applications

The assessment instruments identified in this research were not designed to yield a score or grade. They were designed to measure the overall effectiveness of the encounter. This information could then be used to modify the encounter itself and not rate the students' success or failure. Movies, plays, art galleries, and a host of other out-of-classroom activities can be used as authentic curricula that can provide interesting and motivating learning pathways.

One study featured assessment that was produced by parents interacting with their child. Students were stimulated by their parents' involvement and the students felt comfortable with their parents. Researchers found this type of assessment to suffer from low reliability and validity, but it had its advantages. The collaborative, nonthreatening nature of the informal project fostered active and meaningful learning and an integrated school, home, and community.

It's clear that traditional content assessment may miss the point of the out-of-school experience or informal in-school learning. There is a wider range of attributes and facets that need to be measured, and a content test would send the wrong message to students about what is important. Extending the experience by expanding it with a related performance-based project, writing activity, or other application would be a better gauge of mastery than a traditional test. The author of the research felt that projects with appropriate scoring rubrics, where students combine discipline content from the classroom and the informal experience, are the best way for students to demonstrate this type of learning. Ultimately the teacher wants to facilitate growth of enthusiasm and motivation.

Precautions and Possible Pitfalls

Consider a student who usually performs poorly in the traditional classroom yet exhibits enthusiasm and interest in more hands-on activities and participation in out-of-school learning experiences. This situation presents teachers with a dilemma as to how to encourage students like this and not penalize them with narrow-range, traditional classroom assessment devices. The teacher should not turn the students' enthusiasm off. Balancing opportunities for successful assessment and evaluation gives students in this group more than one pathway to find and demonstrate success. Oral presentations, project display boards, student videos, computer-generated presentations (e.g., PowerPoint), and other instructional outcomes can help these students find success.

Another problem is providing equal access and opportunity for all students in class. Sometimes parental support is not available to all students. The teacher needs to make learning outside the classroom an option with an in-school component for those that can't participate in off-campus activities. In a marine biology class in a high school located near the coast, an intertidal visit and beach walk had an alternative in-class option for those that couldn't get to the beach during low tides.

Sources

Korpan, C. A., Bisanz, G. L., Bisanz, J., Boehme, C., & Lynch, M. A. (1997). What did you learn outside of school today? Using structured interviews to document home and community activities related to science and technology. *Science Education, 81*(6), 651-662.

Kurth, L. A., & Richmond, G. (1999). Moving from outside to inside: High school students' use of apprenticeship as a vehicle for entering the culture and practice of science. *Journal of Research in Science Teaching, 36*(6), 677-697.

Ramsey-Gassert, L. (1997). Learning science beyond the classroom. *Elementary School Journal, 97*(4).

Strategy 44: Keep feedback positive to bolster student confidence.

What the Research Says

In a study focusing on a sophomore honors English class at a public high school in the Midwest, students were asked what types of teacher comments on their writing provided the most help while encouraging them to improve as writers. Not surprisingly, students prefer to see comments worded in a positive manner on their papers. They do not want comments that tell them they have done something wrong without offering them advice on how to correct their mistakes. They want a "response that is courteous and gentle that gives help without threatening the writer's dignity" (Atwell, 1987). This positive feedback can translate to improvement.

At least three studies (Daiker, 1983; Dragga, 1986; Harris, 1977) have shown that teachers usually do not praise students' writing often enough. Daiker, Kerek, and Morenberg (1986) found that the vast majority of comments (89.4%) "cited error or found fault; on . . . 10.6% of them were comments of praise" (p. 104).

Classroom Applications

The goal of student writing is improvement. Therefore, the more specific a teacher can be with comments to students' work with thorough explanations and just deserved praise of what they have done right (as opposed to taking the dreaded red pen and marking only what is wrong), the more likely students will feel supported and will work to improve. We must also look at our own commenting style. Do we comment only on form or do we include content? Do we consider the ideas the student is proposing? If the objective is to improve over several drafts, then certainly grammatical errors such as spelling and punctuation should not formulate the majority of a teacher's comments. These parts of writing are important, but can be revised in a later draft, after the student has the content-oriented problems ironed out. Do we tell students what is right with their work as well as give them a thorough explanation of what needs to be done to correct mistakes?

Telling a student to be more specific has little or no meaning for them if, as a teacher, you do not tell them which part of their text needs to be more specific.

Precautions and Possible Pitfalls

Whether they are writing papers for English, science, or history, most students want their writing to reflect improvement. The teacher needs to be careful not to use praise that is too general or of a patronizing nature. At the beginning of a course the teacher should go over the specific commenting style with students and whether symbols will be used as well as written comments. The teacher should make sure students understand what these symbols mean. In addition to written comments, the teacher should talk to students on a regular basis about their papers and encourage students to ask questions if the comments they are given aren't clear.

Sources

Atwell, N. (1987). "In the middle": Writing, reading, and learning with adolescents. Portsmouth, NH: Boynton/Cook.

Bardine, B. A. (1999). Students' perceptions of written teacher comments: What do they say about how we respond to them? High School Journal, 82(4).

Daiker, D. (1983, March). *The teacher's options in responding to student writing.* Paper presented at the annual conference on College Composition and Communication, Washington, DC.

Daiker, D. A., Kerek, A., & Morenberg, M. (1986). *The writer's options: Combining composing* (3rd ed.). New York: Harper.

Dragga, S. (1986, March). *Praiseworthy grading: A teacher's alternative to editing error.* Paper presented at the Conference on College Composition and Communication, New Orleans.

Harris, W. H. (1977). Teacher response to student writing: A study of the response pattern of high school teachers to determine the basis for teacher judgment of student writing. *Research in the Teaching of English, 11,* 175-185.

Strategy 45: Get beyond marking student responses right or wrong. Students need explicit, detailed feedback about their performance.

What the Research Says

 Feedback is important for students in several ways: it helps them assess their mastery of course material, helps them assess their use of thinking and learning strategies, and helps them connect their efforts and strategies to their academic outcomes. The primary benefit of feedback is the identification of errors of knowledge and understanding and the assistance with correcting those errors. Feedback generally improves subsequent performance on similar items. Research suggests feedback can guide students in their use of learning strategies and that adults who try different strategies and are tested on their learning can generally identify effective strategies (Crooks, 1988).

Classroom Applications

Go beyond simply marking items right or wrong and giving students a score on a test so that students can have better ideas about how they went wrong. Make comments to stimulate students' thinking about their errors. If grading time is a factor, consider oral test reviews. Find ways to reward students to authentically engage in correcting misconceptions and wrong answers. Some disciplines are easier than others to do this with. Also consider a pretest over the same concepts you will cover on the actual test. Reward the students that take the time to correct their mistakes on the pretest. This gives you another teachable moment with the class or individuals. The more motivated students will take advantage of the opportunity.

Precautions and Potential Pitfalls

⚠️ Teachers spend many hours grading papers, writing comments, and giving feedback. However, there is always doubt as to how much students read and internalize the comments after seeing the score. Many students are not concerned with really knowing the test's content and specific concepts. As an alternative, try to structure classtime during activities or quiet assignments to give verbal rather than written feedback. You will receive feedback yourself and get to know your students better.

Source

Crooks, T. (1988). Impact of classroom evaluation practices on students. *Review of Educational Research, 58*(4), 438-481.

 Strategy 46: Move beyond paper to an electronic file cabinet or a digital portfolio as assessment alternatives.

What the Research Says

The Annenberg Institute for School Reform and the Coalition for Essential Schools, with the support of IBM, investigated the use of the digital portfolio at six schools. Digital Portfolio software was used to create a multimedia collection of students' work and connect the work to performance standards. The sites represented rural, suburban, and urban schools that were both technology rich and poor. Digital Portfolio software was customized for each school and part of the effort included putting portfolio content online. In addition to the usual goals and objectives of the portfolio strategy, the aim of the digital portfolio was to expand the viewing audience to include college admissions and placement offices.

Word processing, scanning, and digitizing audio and video provided the means of entry into the multimedia portfolio. Researchers found the need for the targeted schools to support a schoolwide vision on how technology, and digital portfolios in particular, corresponds with the school's other systems. The main benefit of the digital portfolio in contrast to its paper counterpart seems to be its ability to become available to a wider audience. In addition, technology can add a few extra process steps that provide the students greater opportunity to reflect on and polish their presentations.

Classroom Applications

 While a schoolwide digital portfolio requirement might not be realistic or feasible, a digital portfolio option may be just the right thing for specific classes or students. Consider the following ideas:

- Allow motivated and interested students the option of a digital portfolio. Student artists or photographers could benefit by digitizing all their work, along with appropriate reflection and written content.
- Students interested in technology as a career could benefit by recording their mastery in the field as well as fulfilling a specific class portfolio requirement.
- A student could produce a digital job resume in portfolio form.
- Form a class portfolio and turn it into a class Web page that is available to a much wider audience.
- Include parents as collaborators and viewers in digital technology.

Digital media provide another vehicle for sharing student work. Because it is a relatively new idea, the limits of technology have not been reached. Creative students and teachers can experiment with new and innovative uses of the digital portfolio as it finds its niche within other instructional strategies.

Precautions and Possible Pitfalls

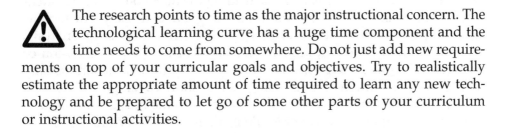 The research points to time as the major instructional concern. The technological learning curve has a huge time component and the time needs to come from somewhere. Do not just add new requirements on top of your curricular goals and objectives. Try to realistically estimate the appropriate amount of time required to learn any new technology and be prepared to let go of some other parts of your curriculum or instructional activities.

Source

Niguidula, D. (1997). Picturing performance with digital portfolios. *Educational Leadership, 55*(3), 26-29.

Strategy 47: Help students embrace their errors for more meaningful instruction. That is the kind of academic feedback that will most help them improve their future performance.

What the Research Says

Teachers often give students less than useful information about their academic performance. Studies have shown that students benefit more from learning about when they are wrong than when they are right. In addition, for students to improve their future performance, they need to know why something is wrong. Research shows that teachers often fail to provide students with this kind of information about their performance. When students understand why something is wrong, they are more likely to learn appropriate strategies to eliminate their errors.

Classroom Applications

Even with the emphasis on high-level thinking skills and teaching processes, in general, there are lots of opportunities for students to give a simple right answer or a wrong response to their answers. For a teacher to merely indicate the right answer, or to indicate that a student's response is wrong, does little to aim the student in the right direction. Teachers should analyze incorrect responses to see if the errors are in reasoning, incorrect interpretations of major concepts, faulty work with the concept details, or problems with the reading the question correctly. Oftentimes, such an analysis can be time-consuming, but extremely worthwhile, for it is the discovery of the error (resulting from their error analysis) that can be the key to helping students sort out their comprehension or learning difficulties. Remember, more meaningful instruction usually contributes to retention of more than just one shot "coverage."

There are several types of errors that occur in the normal curriculum-student interaction in classrooms. First, there are the errors which are common to a large portion of the class. These can be attributable to a misunderstanding in class or to some prior learning common to most of the class that causes students to similarly react incorrectly to a specific situation. When the teacher notices this sort of thing, then a general remark and clarification to the entire class would be appropriate. The misconception may be one of not understanding the details or background behind a concept. Understanding the grammar or math leads to mastery of the concept. Analysis of errors in thinking and quick and instant feedback can turn potential drudgery into pride of understanding.

Wrong answers and misconceptions provide teachable moments and quick feedback opportunities. In this case, rapid feedback is important in your effort to help students avoid the frustration that turns them off. Most of them have had the math but not within an authentic context.

Precautions and Possible Pitfalls

It is possible that, through an error analysis of a student's work, several errors may turn up. To point out too many faults at one time could confound the student and consequently have a counterproductive effect. The teacher should arrange the discovered errors in order of importance and successively discuss them with the student one by one, going on to the next one only after successful completion of the earlier one. Teachers should follow up to see if the students successfully followed their error-correction plans and have rectified previous errors, especially recurring errors.

Source

Bangert-Drowns, R. L., Kulik, C. C., Kulik, J. A., & Morgan, M. (1991). The instructional effect of feedback in test-like events. *Review of Educational Research, 61,* 213-238.

Strategy 48: Remember to use assessment as a teaching and learning opportunity.

What the Research Says

Research shows that tests and other assessment devices can be used to improve learning, rather than just evaluating students' mastery of content. One study compared the test performance of students who took an initial or pretest with those who did not take an initial test. The results showed that students who took the initial test did better than those who did not, indicating that they actually learned from the test experience (Foos & Fisher, 1988).

Assessment is most effective when it also includes students' self-monitoring and self-evaluating so that they can regulate or manage their own learning. One way of promoting students' ability to self-assess their performance is through error analysis (Hartman, 2001). Research on teaching students to use such strategies demonstrates that students need to be able to answer the following self-questions about such a strategy before it is used effectively in a variety of situations and tasks (Schunk, 2000).

1. *What is error analysis?* It's a systematic approach for using feedback metacognitively to improve one's future performance. It involves obtaining strategic metacognitive knowledge about one's mistakes and recycling that knowledge for self-improvement.

2. *When and why is it used?* Error analysis has several potential benefits. First, it gives students a second opportunity to master important material. Second, it develops students' metacognition, both strategic knowledge and executive management, as students evaluate their test performance, identify errors and possible error patterns, and plan for the future. For example, it can help students anticipate their specific likely errors and self-correct them before turning in a test. Third, it helps internalize students' attributions so that they recognize that their educational outcomes (grades) are a result of their own efforts, actions, and strategies, factors within their control. This is in contrast to attributing their performance to external factors outside their control, such as the professor or bad luck. This could improve students' feelings of self-efficacy, their academic self-concept in the specific subject area, and perhaps transfer to their general academic self-concept. Thus, error analysis improves critical thinking abilities of self-monitoring and self-evaluating one's own performance and can improve students' feelings about their ability to succeed in your discipline.

3. How is an error analysis performed? Error analysis requires identifying the correct information, answer, and approach and identifying what errors, omissions, and so on were made, determining why they occurred, and planning how to prevent them in the future. When performing error analyses, students should (1) identify what their wrong answer was and what the correct answer is (declarative knowledge); (2) determine specifically why they got the answer wrong (contextual knowledge); and (3) formulate an action plan on how they have now learned and understand the material and how they will remember this information (procedural knowledge).

Error Analysis Model

1. What answer I had AND what the answer really was. OR What I did wrong AND what I should have done.

2. Why did I choose the wrong answer? OR Why did I do it wrong?

3. How will I remember what I now know is the correct answer? OR How will I make sure I don't make the same mistake again?

In all three steps the student must focus on the specific content involved in the error rather than focus on general causes of errors.

Pelley and Dalley's (1997) question analysis is intended to help students make a broader analysis of test questions than just a literal interpretation because a narrower, more literal interpretation can constrain their studying and limit learning. Their procedure has four steps: identifying topics, understanding the correct answer, understanding wrong answers, and rephrasing the question. Pelley and Dalley encourage students to ask questions such as, "How would I have had to study to know that the correct answer was right?" "How would I have had to study to know that each wrong answer was wrong?" Focusing on the topic rather than the question helps students understand material more deeply, so they understand how ideas are interrelated, and therefore students are able to correctly answer more and different questions.

Classroom Applications

 The following are examples of error analysis on a biology multiple-choice test item and on a research report (Hartman, 2001).

Multiple-Choice Item

Question

Which of the following is the correct characterization for the *resting* membrane potential of a typical neuron?

(a) It is negative outside compared to inside.

(b) It depends on high permeability of the membrane to sodium and potassium ions.

(c) It carries impulses from one region to another.

(d) It results from the unequal distribution of ions across the membrane.

Error Analysis of Item

1. What I got wrong and what the right answer is: I thought the answer was "b", but now I know the answer is "d".

2. Why I got it wrong: I know there was high permeability to potassium but I forgot it was impermeable to sodium.

3.   How I will remember this and prevent future similar mistakes: I'll remember that the resting potential of a neuron depends upon the *imbalance*. The unequal distribution of ions results from the difference in permeability between sodium and potassium. The membrane is highly permeable to potassium, but it is impermeable to sodium. This causes it to be negative inside compared to the outside. I'll also try to use the process of elimination more so I can rule out some of the answer choices.

Alternative Error Analysis

1.   What I got wrong and what I should have done: I lost credit because I did not properly cite all of the sources of my information in the text and on the reference list at the end. I should have put the authors' last names and publication years in the body of the report where I discussed them in addition to their names on the list at the end of the report. All names have to be in both places; I had some in one place but not the other.

2.   Why I did this wrong: In high school we didn't have to do this so I didn't know it was the correct procedure. I didn't understand "plagiarism". I also didn't read the assignment sheet carefully enough to see this was required. I just read it to get a general idea of what was expected and missed some of the details.

3.   How I will prevent similar mistakes in the future: I'll remember to cite my sources in the text because I'll think about how I would feel if someone took my ideas and didn't give me credit for them. I'll also read my assignment sheets more carefully, looking for specific details instead of general ideas. Finally, I'll use a checklist to make sure I really do everything I plan to do. The checklist will have two sections for each thing I have to do. One section will be to track my progress; the other will be to rate the quality of the work I've done.

Precautions and Potential Pitfalls

Students historically have differing degrees of difficulty with different parts of an error analysis. The first question, about what students got wrong and what the right answer is, tends to be relatively easy for students. The second question, requiring students to explain why they erred, is moderately difficult, especially when it comes to specifics. Students try to get away with general excuses such as "I didn't study enough" instead of making specific analyses of why their lack of sufficient studying caused them to make the particular error they made. The third question, about how students will use what they learned to improve their future performance, is the most difficult for students. Developing retention strategies and learning improvement plans requires hard and sustained thinking.

Sources

Foos, P. W., & Fisher, R. P. (1988). Using tests as learning opportunities. *Journal of Educational Psychology, 80*(2), 179-183.

Hartman, H. (2001). Developing students' metacognitive knowledge and strategies. In H. Hartman (Ed.), *Metacognition in learning and instruction: Theory, research, and practice* (pp. 69-83). Dordrecht, The Netherlands: Kluwer.

Pelley, J. W., & Dalley, B. K. (1997). *Successful types for medical students.* Lubbock, TX: Texas Tech University Extended Learning.

Schunk, D. (2000). *Learning theories: An educational perspective* (3rd ed.). Upper Saddle River, NJ: Merrill.

Strategy 49: Look beyond test scores by keeping a range of student work. Using student portfolios to collect more substantive evidence of your curriculum and teaching initiatives allows you to compare, contrast, and counteract narrowly defined test scores.

What the Research Says

Reflections over a 10-year period explored the many teaching and learning experiences involving portfolio assessment. Timely and careful assessment and evaluation painted a clear picture of what portfolios are and what portfolios aren't. Influenced by Howard Gardner's multiple intelligences, the faculty of Crow Island School in Winnetka, Illinois, assessed and evaluated their 10-year journey and the evolution of their portfolio thinking. Overall, they found portfolios fulfilled the promises they felt portfolios held when they began. The staff defined and refined the roles of all stakeholders in the portfolio concept and today continue to gain a more in-depth view of their students as learners through the use of the their full site-based, student-centered portfolio vision.

Classroom Applications

Points to consider when thinking about portfolios:

1. Portfolios in education, by most definitions, are created to tell a story. Don't be too rigid when deciding what goes into one. Consider allowing and helping the students to decide what goes into the "story" of

their learning and growth. Are the portfolios going to be teacher-centered or student-centered? Who decides what goes into one?

2.   Decide what work will go home and what should stay in the portfolio. Are you presenting parents a "chapter" at a time or are you presenting a more temporal view within the portfolio paradigm?

3.   Whose portfolio is it? Should you assume the role of a portfolio manager and let students decide what will counterbalance test scores and enter the portfolio? If you decide to do it this way, help the students in their decisions. You are developing competent and thoughtful storytellers. When students are first discovering what a portfolio is, they require a scaffolding strategy.

4.   Grading or attaching a letter grade to a portfolio seems to run contrary to the nature of the concept. Give it some thought.

5.   Select a timeframe for the history of the learning a portfolio might represent. Is a portfolio a year's worth of work?

6.   For some students "telling" a long-term story is too abstract. Defining an audience for the work contributes to a more concrete picture.

7.   Attach meaning to each piece in a portfolio by asking students to write a short reason for its inclusion into the story. "Reflection tag" was the term used in the research literature. This contributes to the student's metacognitive growth and attaches further value and meaning to the individual content.

8.   Deliberately teach parents about the value of student portfolios: what they mean to you, the curriculum, and the students.

Precautions and Possible Pitfalls

On the surface, portfolios sound like a simple concept. Do not underestimate the learning curve for teachers, students, and parents if the concept is to really function at its best. Expect some frustration during the implementation and transition to portfolio adoption.

Source

Hebert, E. (1998). Lessons learned about student portfolios. *Phi Delta Kappan,* 79(8), 583-585.

6

Working With Special Needs Students

 Strategy 50: Make yourself aware of the wide range of specific factors associated with underachievement. This can help you to consider intervention plans more precisely and effectively.

What the Research Says

This study surveyed over 100 articles over a 20-year period and identified some 41 factors related to student underachievement. The range of factors included community and cultural influences, family and peer interactions, and behaviors in the educational setting that interfered with teaching and learning. From this list, researchers then narrowed the number of variables, by peer and professional review and consensus, to the top 10 influences.

The study focused its efforts on meeting the needs of diverse student populations in urban schools and then made research-based recommendations for school personnel. These recommendations or interventions included instructional strategies, methods of image building, and changes in the behaviors of academic professionals. Their goal was to be able to focus in on the key variables related to underachievement and to make specific recommendations for school personnel in assisting underachieving urban students.

Classroom Applications

Most new teachers come from a background of success as students in the way they have experienced the institution of education. In fact they liked it so much they wanted to be part of it and worked very hard to return to the classroom as teachers! From this perspective, teachers, especially new teachers, have a difficult time understanding why certain students don't feel the same way about the classroom, learning, and school as they do. Underachievement can be outside a new teacher's personal paradigm. Not understanding where an underachieving student is coming from frequently leads to teacher confusion, frustration, and avoidance of the student and the problem.

It is also common for many teachers, as they become more experienced and acquire a little political power within their school, to try to isolate themselves from underachieving students rather than try to work with them. However, with insight, reflection, empathy, and effort, you can gain some confidence in your ability to be successful with traditionally underachieving student groups. Information about the possible causes along with a willingness to try to understand and create educational strategies can go a long way toward professional and personal fulfillment. The consensus of the 10 top influences, reviewed by experts in student underachievement and students at risk for failure, is listed here. All school personnel need to consider and act on these 10 top influences.

1. *Teacher behavior* refers to the teacher's actions that demonstrate care, respect, and interest in the personal, as well as academic, growth of their students.

2. *Teacher expectations* for students' achievement of realistic academic standards are directly or indirectly communicated to students and usually result in the students' attainment of those standards.

3. *Curriculum relevance* refers to the students' perceptions of how meaningful and usable the content material and the instructional methods are in their personal lives.

4. *Class size* is the number of students enrolled in a classroom.

5. *Disengagement* from school-related activities pertains to the lack of student involvement in and identification with the school community.

6. *Confidence in the students' ability to achieve* refers to the students' belief and expectation that they can learn academic material and be successful in school.

7. *High mobility* in school attendance or a transferring from one school to another can cause both students and parents to feel alone and disconnected from the new school or school environment.

8. *Parental expectations and involvement* refers to the parents' realistic academic performance standards and goals for their children as well as their active engagement in meeting those goals.

9. *Level of parents' education* is the number of years parents have been involved in formal education as well as their level of academic accomplishments (e.g., high school graduation, bachelor's degree).

10. *Poverty or low income* (e.g., annual family income falling below poverty standards) often creates conditions in the family that, if uncorrected, could result in student underachievement.

While the study goes on to identify specific strategies to mitigate these influences, it concluded with three particularly noteworthy findings that emerged from threads connecting all 10 influences, which are summarized here:

● First, engagement level and expectations for success are critical not only for students but for school personnel and parents as well. The more confident all parties are in their ability to overcome barriers, the greater the chance for success. Past successes should be invoked as evidence that challenges can be overcome.

● Second, high mobility and attendance problems created learning and teaching environments characterized by disconnection and feelings of being alone. The effects of this relate to not only the students, but also the parents and the school community as a whole. Schools can take positive steps to decrease the negative influence of mobility by inviting parents and students to become more involved and take a more active part in the school community.

● Third, school personnel have more influence over some conditions associated with chronic underachievement (e.g., teacher behaviors and expectations, curriculum relevance) than over others (e.g., low income of parents). The researchers found that school personnel could proactively address problems caused by some of the influences that they may not be able to control directly. Creating an environment where parents are included as vital members of the team was cited in numerous studies.

Most of the recommendations offered by the study involved a change in the strategies used by counselors, tutoring services, parent organizations, and caring teachers, systems already in place. Personnel need to use these traditional resources to address the common influences related to under-achievement. Their study indicated that there was little need to develop new systems.

Precautions and Possible Pitfalls

⚠️ No system or program will replace a single caring and involved teacher. This starts with one teacher dealing professionally and emotionally with one student at a time. This is done with the help, input, and insight of support services and other caring and insightful school personnel and the student's family. Also, be aware that not every family or family member will be useful in mitigating the student's problems. Some are the source of the problems.

It can't be emphasized enough that this is a team effort. Gather all the information you can from others that know the student or students before acting. Make sure other experienced school personnel know what you are doing and whom you are working with. This strategy can go a long way in helping you avoid the potential pitfalls that are ingrained in student interventions.

Source

Arroyo, A., Rhoad, R., & Drew, P. (1999). Meeting diverse student needs in urban schools: Research-based recommendations for school improvement. *Preventing School Failure, 43*(4) 145-153.

Strategy 51: Support the needs of challenged students with a team effort. Find opportunities to collaborate and coteach with special education colleagues as well as other school professionals who have expertise in this area.

What the Research Says

Veteran teachers realize the benefits of collaborating with colleagues to problem solve and troubleshoot. In today's classrooms, the challenges new teachers face in trying to meet the educational, social, and emotional needs of diverse learners can be overwhelming. Teacher educators are increasingly realizing the benefits of teamwork. With school reform and restructuring, and the "least restrictive environment" practice taking the spotlight, coplanning and coteaching may provide powerful ways to address the demands of students with special needs (Hafernick, Messerschmitt, & Vandrick, 1997). Many schools are now using the model of coteaching for their special needs population. In this model the general education and special education teachers coteach in the same classrooms.

In a 1999 study by Duchardt, Marlow, Inman, Christensen, and Reeves, the special education faculty of a university in Louisiana initiated collaborative opportunities with the general education faculty for coplanning and coteaching. Teachers met once a week, over lunch, to discuss course content and lesson delivery. As an outgrowth of these meetings, meeting participants developed a coplanning and coteaching model to assist other educators who wished to collaborate. A step-by-step design of this model follows.

- Stage 1. Choose a trusted teacher with whom to collaborate. Obstacles can result when misunderstandings or miscommunications occur. The goal of collaboration is clear: success for special education students. The more this goal is discussed and used as a motivating factor, the more trust can be established and the greater the rapport that is generated.

- Stage 2. Find pockets of time to plan. Carve out small blocks of time in the beginning to meet with other team members to discuss course content. Down the road, planning can occur on an as-needed basis, or even by phone or e-mail.

- Stage 3. Brainstorm! After discussing course content, team members can brainstorm options for coteaching the lesson. Brainstorming helps establish the expertise of each team member and permits planning to advance easily and without delay.

- Stage 4. Prepare the actual lesson. The team members discuss, prepare, and develop a written guide for coteaching the lesson. Consider having the lesson videotaped to assess and amend the lesson plan for future use.

- Stage 5. Coteach the lesson. The first time a lesson is cotaught, the two teachers must test the new instructional strategies. At this point, the preparation time will be obvious in its value. Until the lesson is taught, the teachers will have no idea if the first four strategies are working or if additional strategies for coteaching will be needed. Once the lesson is done, the teachers can evaluate its success.

- Stage 6. Support your team members. A necessary skill for the effective teacher to possess is the capability to be flexible and add to or emphasize key points throughout the lesson. Each team member needs to establish a comfortable and secure working relationship as well as trust in the intentions of the other team members.

• Stage 7. Assess the lesson. After the lesson is presented, each team member can provide the presenting teacher with feedback. If the lesson was videotaped, team members can view the ways in which the lesson can be improved or polished. Having other trusted colleagues view the lesson might also provide valuable insights.

According to the study by Duchardt et al., coplanning and coteaching arrangements can result in nine positive outcomes:

1. Collaboration and development of trust

2. Learning to be flexible and collegial

3. Finding pockets of time to coplan

4. Learning through trial and error

5. Forming teaching and learning partnerships

6. Challenging ourselves and developing professionally

7. Solving problems as a team

8. Meeting the needs of diverse learners

9. Meeting the needs of teachers as problem solvers

Classroom Applications

The African proverb "it takes a village to raise a child" can be adapted in education today to read, "It takes the whole school to educate a child." With the needs of special education students and other diverse learners, coplanning and coteaching offer students (and teachers) opportunities for success. The collaboration between general education teachers, special education teachers, school counselors, speech therapists, and other school professionals can make a critical difference in helping students with special needs achieve.

In one West Coast high school this model has been used extremely effectively. Taking a team approach has resulted in greater collaboration among all the staff members. The coteaching model is so successful that other districts have come to observe and talk to participating teachers. General education teachers feel supported when dealing with their special needs students and special education teachers can assist their students in succeeding in mainstream classes.

Precautions and Possible Pitfalls

 While more and more schools are using a team approach when dealing with special needs students, caution should be taken. Team members must be committed to making this model work. Each member of the team provides expertise and insights critical to the success of students involved. Also, general education teachers sometimes aren't used to team teaching and may feel uncomfortable having another teacher in their classrooms. Coteaching should be just that. The special education teacher should not become an aide for the general education teacher but an integral part of the lesson. This is where planning is of critical importance.

Sources

Duchardt, B., Marlow, L., Inman, D., Christensen, P., & Reeves, M. (1999). Collaboration and co-teaching: General and special education faculty. *Clearing House, 72*(3) (Special Section: Culture and the Schools), 186-191.

Hafernick, J. J., Messerschmitt, D. S., & Vandrick, S. (1997). Collaborative research: Why and how? *Educational Researcher, 26*(9), 31-35.

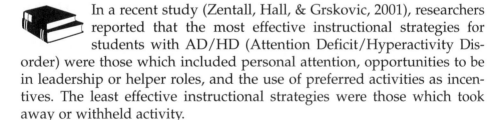

Strategy 52: Tap the strengths of students with Attention Deficit/Hyperactivity Disorder (ADHD) with effective instructional strategies.

What the Research Says

In a recent study (Zentall, Hall, & Grskovic, 2001), researchers reported that the most effective instructional strategies for students with AD/HD (Attention Deficit/Hyperactivity Disorder) were those which included personal attention, opportunities to be in leadership or helper roles, and the use of preferred activities as incentives. The least effective instructional strategies were those which took away or withheld activity.

Classroom Applications

 The frustrations of beginning teachers dealing with lesson planning, state testing schedules, classroom management, managing the paper load, and just trying to find enough hours in the day to accomplish it all can be overwhelming. Add to these responsibilities students with special needs (such as AD/HD) and new teachers may feel like they are navigating in choppy seas.

For a beginning teacher working with a special needs student, the first person to seek out for support can be a veteran special education teacher who has a thorough understanding of the student's IEP (individual education plan). Using special education teachers to help plan activities and lessons can be a tremendous resource for the new teacher. They can also provide helpful hints in dealing with discipline issues, preferential seating, and the importance of presenting clear, specific, and simple directions.

Stimulation through social interactions and activity-based lessons has been found to be effective with special needs students. Teachers should avoid lengthy doses of seat time and sedentary work. The use of hands-on and manipulative activities is also more effective with special needs students and may enable them to be successful. Providing the student with opportunities to move around the classroom can also be helpful. Allowing the student to run an errand, hand out papers, clean the board, or help out in the classroom can help reinforce appropriate behavior.

Because students with AD/HD may experience greater difficulty in starting and organizing tasks, the teacher should consider breaking assignments down into smaller pieces while remembering to check for understanding at regular intervals.

Precautions and Possible Pitfalls

Having a student with special needs in class can be challenging for any teacher. If the teacher is organized and has straightforward and concise classroom rules and procedures, with consequences clearly stated, the chances for student success increase. Teachers need to be sensitive to students with special needs and not announce to the class that "John" is allowed extra time on an assignment because of his disability. Most students with special needs don't want attention drawn to them. Any modifications that are discussed with a student should be done in a one-on-one setting away from other students.

Source

Zentall, S. S., Hall, A. M., & Grskovic, J. A. (2001). Learning and motivational characteristics of boys with AD/HD and/or giftedness. *Exceptional Children, 67*(4), 419-519.

Strategy 53: Use project-based learning activities to help at risk students succeed.

What the Research Says

Teachers of at risk students tend to focus on basic skills, using traditional instructional methods such as whole-group lecture, repetitive drill-and-practice, and simple remedial exercises (Means, Chelmer, & Knapp, 1991). Students find these methods, when used almost exclusively, to be uninteresting, often resulting in reduced educational opportunities for the at risk students. At risk students are often not given the opportunities to learn using the advanced skills needed for problem solving and critical thinking.

Educational research indicates that project-based learning activities can help at risk students learn and practice a variety of skills and improve their attitudes toward learning (Duttweiler, 1992; Means, 1994).

Classroom Applications

To increase chances for at risk students to be successful in class, while also providing skills needed for problem solving and critical thinking, teachers need to provide opportunities to participate in interesting and challenging project-based learning. The most beneficial project-based learning activities include six characteristics (Duttweiler, 1992; Means, 1994):

1. Opportunities to explore domains of interest

2. Active, interactive, and attractive instruction

3. Project orientation

4. Collaboration with peers

5. Opportunities to act as learner as well as designer

6. Opportunities to practice and develop fluency for advanced skills

By integrating technology with the curriculum, students have the chance to use technology to become more prepared for the job market as well as the demands of real life. The Web provides many sites with specific technology-based lessons prepared for students. Giving students choices, within project guidelines, allows for more student buy-in, practice in time management and organization, and a sense of ownership and empowerment. By teaming at risk students in groups, there is a greater chance for collaboration, self-esteem, and teamwork. Integrating project-based opportunities can provide students an effective instructional strategy for improving their chances of success.

Precautions and Potential Pitfalls

Care should be taken to make sure technology-based projects provide students the opportunities to browse diverse sources of information. The teacher should consult with knowledgeable colleagues and ask for their recommendations for projects. This way they can be age and ability appropriate, and use academically relevant content. Do not rush to implement project-based activities without careful planning.

Sources

Duttweiler, P. C. (1992). Engaging at-risk students with technology. *Media and Methods, 29*(2), 6-8.

Means, B. (1994). Using technology to advance educational goals. In B. Means (Ed.), *Technology in educational reform: The reality behind the promise*. San Francisco: Jossey-Bass.

Means, B., Chelmer, C., & Knapp, M. S. (1991). *Teaching advanced skills to at-risk students: Views from research and practice*. San Francisco: Jossey-Bass.

7

Celebrating Diversity in the Classroom: Emphasizing the Positive in Cultural, Linguistic, Ethnic, and Gender Identity

 Strategy 54: Expect a wide range of working conditions, as all schools and school districts are not created equal. Preservice, student, or new bilingual teachers need to be prepared for

a potentially diverse range of expectations, from both a curricular and a local political standpoint, from school to school and district to district.

What the Research Says

This study examined the numerous perceptions of 20 bilingual teachers in Southern California, in the post-Proposition 227, 1998-1999 school year. The proposition calls for English-only instructional programs with the goal of total immersion being the most effective method to learn English. The introduction points out various examples of a long history of conflict and sometimes chaos in the way non-English-speaking immigrants were taught English and generally assimilated into the educational mainstream. While the research and Proposition 227 are based in California, 17 other states are dealing with other forms of English-only legislation, laws, or guidelines. The researcher states many bilingual teachers are seen as "marginal teachers" who must teach those "foreigners" who refuse to learn English. This then contributes to the bilingual teacher feeling isolated, alienated, and under intense scrutiny.

In-depth interviews and a questionnaire produced data to hopefully shed light on the following themes:

1. The subject's rationale for the advantages and importance of bilingual education

2. Whether their students had experienced any academic setbacks resulting from Proposition 227

3. Parents' reaction to the initiative

4. Parents' rights

5. Any notable changes in attitudes of nonbilingual teachers and staff toward them and their students

6. The extent to which they had followed guidelines or used loopholes to engage in resistance behavior

The stories told by teachers in the study were of beliefs, values, frustrations, challenges, and ethical and curricular dilemmas they encountered in teaching language-minority students. Overall these teachers reported that Proposition 227 had created chaos, confusion, and academic setbacks for students and had intensified animosity between bilingual and nonbilingual advocates.

Respondents did show resilience and continued commitment to bilingual education and saw a role change to facilitators of reorganization. The teachers in this study also showed resistance and contestation behaviors to the mandates.

They understood the hostile environment created by Proposition 227 and acted as insulators and protectors for their students.

Classroom Applications

In a typical staff dynamic, certain teachers emerge as leaders and zealous advocates for their programs and their students. This is accomplished usually by shear force of professional personality within a teaching staff. These leaders make it a point to line up administrators, both at their school and at the district level, with parents and community leaders behind them. The resulting formal and informal power base works to cement a program together and creates a resiliency that protects and maintains their program. This type of presence, within a staff, changes minds and goes a long way in placing their program in a positive light. Not every new teacher is capable of establishing this type of program aura, however.

New teachers need to realize that most good, effective programs are the result of individuals. These individuals didn't just fall into the program, *they are the program,* and if they leave, some or maybe all their power and the program may go too or at least drastically change.

As a part of a potentially marginalized educational program, you can make a difference. However, the playing field, as presented in the research, is not even for bilingual programs. Understanding the politics at your site, regionally, and at the state level is an important start. The origin of your problems comes from both inside and outside the classroom.

The teachers' students, curriculum, and pedagogy do need to be their first priority, but the job requires teachers to do more. Teachers will need to advocate for the resources and an equal standing for their program within the power structure of the school institution. Unlike other content teachers, bilingual teachers will need to do more and often deal with more frustration and face greater challenges than their counterparts.

Empowering limited or non-English speakers is a noble and necessary act. It is part of a long thread that connects the history of the United States. There is a rich history of language-minority students who have benefited and contributed socially, economically, educationally, and culturally. School has always been a source of socialization strategies for language-minority students. However, career bilingual teachers need to understand going in how public and professional sentiments shape and often send confusing and frustrating messages to those in the trenches.

Precautions and Possible Pitfalls

For a new bilingual teacher coming out of college or a university, school culture shock can set a lifelong view of school or teaching. It is important to realize that there are huge differences among schools and districts in the treatment of bilingual programs. If teachers happen to land in bad programs or find themselves working with bitter or burned-out teachers, they must realize that there is a bigger world out there. Be an informed consumer: the teacher can look for positive potential working environments. Teachers should do their homework in gathering as much information as they can before applying for a job in a district.

Sources

Balderrama, M. V. (2001). The (mis)preparation of teachers in the Proposition 227 era: Humanizing teacher roles and their practice. *Urban Review, 33*(3), 255-267.

Valdez, E. O. (2001). Winning the battle, losing the war: Bilingual teachers and post-Proposition 227. *Urban Review, 33*(3), 237-253.

Strategy 55: Think beyond content, as English-language learners come with a variety of challenges and needs.

What the Research Says

This research and reflection centers on the fact that one in four California students is an English-language learner. It also reflects on the fact that 90% of teachers in California are monolingual English speakers. This article examines how legislation and institutionalized practices affect teacher preparation in forcing teachers to accept roles emphasizing a standards-driven, technical, one-size-fits-all approach in addressing the very complex and diverse needs of English-language learners.

Focusing in on California, the researcher (Balderrama, 2001) shows little faith in the ability of California's teacher certification programs to prepare teachers for meeting the needs of English-language learners or immigrant students. Critical review of credentialing practices in California range from the Cross-cultural Language and Academic Development Credential (CLAD) and California Basic Educational Skills Test (CBEST) to Reading in California (RICA) and the California Commission on Teacher Credentialing performance standards. She cites that standards or examinations don't provide any opportunity for examination of the role of the teacher in the socialization and schooling of youth. They tend to dance around the importance of culturally responsive teaching while de-emphasizing the more qualitative and affective aspects of teaching.

In an apparent conflict are the standards-based assessment of good teaching and the more humanized standards most adults use to reflect on how they remember good teachers. In the end it is the humanity that is emphasized in reflection, not teaching methods, techniques, or implementing standards.

Concluding, the paper presents a context of teacher preparation with an emphasis on techniques and standards that tends to misprepare teachers in addressing the needs of an increasingly immigrant student population. The fear is that this mispreparation will in turn misprepare the students academically.

Classroom Applications

Teacher education programs are ideologically based and teachers need to understand the ideological underpinnings that tend to perpetuate social and economic subordination. Find a balance in your role as a teacher from a technical perspective and sometimes, more important, a humanistic perspective.

When dealing with limited English proficiency students or English-language learners, you will find that content and standards can be some of the least important things that you teach and they learn in their lives. Balderamma (2001) states:

> In my attempts to raise the pedagogical consciousness of teachers, together we examine two elements of their teaching: 1) their students, within a historical context, and 2) the context of schooling and teaching. That is, students, particularly English-language learners, must be seen up close, not abstractly, so that understanding of their individual, academic and learning needs are humanized and thus fully understood.

Include a critical understanding of a sociocultural context in your instruction and also use it to help guide your practices.

This type of teaching doesn't call on you to abandon all mandated guidelines, content standards, or expectations; it only asks you to find a larger and more relevant context for them within a larger picture of your students' lives.

Precautions and Possible Pitfalls

Beginning teachers need to be careful to "take the pulse" of their workplace. Colleagues may be under great pressure to raise test scores and student academic achievement. It would be a mistake for teachers to ignore or neglect their responsibility to support school or department goals. However, a teacher can create a more humanistic educational environment in which the teacher and students function. A teacher will be expected to be accountable, but that doesn't mean a teacher can't begin to explore a more humanistic approach to teaching and learning.

Sources

Balderrama, M. V. (2001). The (mis)preparation of teachers in the Proposition 227 era: Humanizing teacher roles and their practice. *Urban Review, 33*(3), 255-267.
Valdez, E. O. (2001). Winning the battle, losing the war: Bilingual teachers and post-Proposition 227. *Urban Review, 33*(3), 237-253.

Strategy 56: Reflect on and promote a positive ethnic identity, as all cultures add value to schools and society. We have experienced huge changes in the ethnic and cultural fabric of our schools, making it essential that Latino and other non-Caucasian teacher ethnicities be reflected in developing and promoting positive ethnic identities for students.

What the Research Says

This research focused on Latino teachers only, yet it makes it clear that the research has meaning for other ethnicities as well. The purpose of this preliminary study was to examine and explore ethnic identity and self-concept as they relate to preservice Latino bilingual teachers. Further, it began to answer questions that relate to relationships and school success within groups of language minority students. It proposed that a teacher with a strong and well-defined ethnic identity could have an effect on the academic success of students.

Multicultural contemporary classrooms now provoke issues such as the construction of racial and ethnic identities, gender roles, and socioeconomic status of students. Within this mix falls a teacher's sense of ethnic identity. Thus, teachers must be aware of the ways in which language, culture, and ethnicity mediate the social constructs of identity. How teachers perceive and interact with these constructs may affect the expectations teachers have for their students. In this study of Latino teachers and Latino students, the basic assumption made is that there is a correlation between how bilingual or ethnically diverse teachers perceive themselves and how they relate to their students. In comparing white, black, and Chicano self-conceptions, Hurstfield (1978) concluded that ethnic membership and status often determine an individual's self-description. Minority subjects were more likely than majority subjects to be conscious of racial or ethnic identity. The research cited past research that found connections between minority teachers sorting out and interpreting their cultural identity and those connections playing a critical role in their identity as educators. Carried further, they found connections between self-concept and teacher efficacy and empowerment.

The direct questions identified for this study were:

- How do bilingual teachers identify themselves ethnically and what are their self-conceptualizations?
- Is there a within-group difference in how these Latino teachers identify themselves?

The subjects for this study were Latino students, mostly Mexican-American, in a bilingual teacher education program at a major university in Texas. Ethnic identity as a psychological construct was established using an open-ended questionnaire.

First, analysis revealed that, for minorities, ethnic self-identification is an individual conceptualization. It is reflected in the heterogeneity found within groups, and ethnic labels are not always interchangeable. Second, it was important that individuals identify themselves too often as individuals who are stereotypically lumped together. Third, patterns with groups can be revealed. These three categories can be used to increase understanding of distinctiveness within minority groups. For example, some U.S.-born individuals identified themselves as Mexican even though they were not foreign born. Ethnic identity can often reflect how individuals recognize the sociopolitical context in which they live.

This limited study produced a variety of recommendations geared toward teacher education programs recognizing the need for minority teachers to struggle with questions regarding their teacher and ethnic identities. Above all, education programs need to address and value the cultural knowledge that minority teachers bring with them. They also need to recognize that their identity as educators will affect many areas of their interaction with students. Sometimes, this identity and cross-cultural literacy will mean more than their content knowledge in other areas of their teacher preparation.

Classroom Applications

 Like expectations you hold for your teaching and learning environments, teacher education programs should value cultural knowledge and provide you with the skills necessary to enhance the ethnic identities of your future students. Because today's classrooms, more than ever, are cross-cultural environments, successful teaching is dependent on positive self-esteem. Ultimately, the way the school and its teachers respond to and support difference affects the degree of school success for many ethnic- and language-minority students.

What this all means is a very personal thing. If you are from a minority culture, how you identify with your culture or how you are seen culturally by your students affects the teaching and learning environment. The research did identify a very heterogeneous mix of cultural self-concepts even within small ethnic groups. Not everyone wants ethnic or cultural background to be subjected to reflection or called attention to. Individuals will have to decide for themselves how their ethnic identity or cultural background becomes or doesn't become an element in their professional lives.

The purpose of the study was to explore ethnic identity and self-concept as they related to preservice Latino teachers and to examine this relationship in regard to the school success of language-minority students. The researchers recommended that teacher education programs help minority preservice teachers with reflection on how they view themselves in the cultural or ethnic mix. Then they can decide how they see themselves as an ethnic person and how it all fits professionally in their teaching.

If a teacher's program didn't or doesn't provide this type of support, the teachers may be on their own in this exploration. A teacher should consider talking to trusted colleagues about the issues or seeking out additional academic research on the topic. There are no easy answers as the individualistic nature of self-ethnic identification doesn't foster one-size-fits-all solutions and strategies.

Ultimately, some will see their calling as role models or advocates for their ethnic or cultural background and for English-language-minority or ethnic-minority students. Others will take the path of assimilation and not want their ethnic and cultural background to be an element in their teaching. Just becoming aware of the choices you have is a start.

Precautions and Possible Pitfalls

There are no real pitfalls in reflecting on these issues. However, the issues can be frustrating. There are no right answers that fill every individual need. Some native Spanish speakers claim that English immersion is the best way to treat English-language learners. Others are passionate advocates for various forms of bilingual education.

Teachers who were once language-minority students may be tempted to feel that the path personally taken toward success in school was the best one. The teachers' expectations for their students could be biased by their personal experiences. The strategy that a teacher experienced may or may not be in touch with current thinking and educational research. The best that can be said is that teachers have options to consider in how they perceive themselves, the identity they want to project as a teacher, and how all this fits into their own teaching and professional relationships.

Sources

Clark, E. R., & Flores, B. B. (2001). Who am I? The social construction of ethnic identity and the self-perceptions in Latino pre-service teachers. *Urban Review*, *33*(2), 69-86.

Clark, E. R., Nystrom, N., & Perez, B. (1996). Language and culture: Critical components of multicultural teacher education. *Urban Review*, *28*, 185-197.

Hurstfield, J. (1978). Internal colonialism: White, black, and chicano self-conceptions. *Ethnic and Racial Studies*, *1*, 6-79.

Strategy 57: Develop multicultural connections in your discipline.

What the Research Says

Making connections when learning mathematics is one of the underlying themes of the National Council of Teachers of Mathematics' (NCTM) Curriculum and Evaluation Standards. Students should be able to connect what they learn in mathematics with problems that arise in different subjects and with multicultural aspects of our society. Five dimensions of multicultural education have been identified as comprising a framework for mathematics:

1. *Integrate content* reflecting diversity when teaching key concepts.

2. *Construct knowledge* so students understand how peoples' points of view within a discipline influence the conclusions they reach.

3. *Reduce prejudice* so students develop positive attitudes toward different groups of people.

4. *Use instructional techniques* that will promote achievement from diverse groups of students.

5. *Modify the school culture* to ensure that people from diverse groups are empowered and have educational equality.

Classroom Applications

Teachers should take into consideration that disciplines and content areas are not free of cultural influences, that some textbooks have racist biases, and that the history of any discipline should not just be viewed from a Eurocentric perspective (Pugh, 1990). Examples of how to apply the five multicultural dimensions to science include the following:

• *Integrate content* so that the history of the discipline's content knowledge comes from many cultures and ethnicities. For example, teach students about George Washington Carver, an African American who made major contributions that influence botany, agribusiness, and biotechnology.

• *Construct knowledge* so students see the universal nature of the components, concepts, and processes of your discipline and how other cultures and ethnic backgrounds might view them.

• *Reduce prejudice* by using teaching and learning that eliminate stereotypes. For example, balance the contributions of Caucasians with other ethnic backgrounds and cultures.

• *Use instructional techniques* that motivate students and demonstrate mutual respect for cultures. For example, group students from diverse cultures for cooperative learning activities, encourage all students to participate in extracurricular activities, and have high expectations for success from all students, regardless of diverse cultural backgrounds. Assign African American students to be tutors with white or Asian students as tutees.

• *Modify the school culture* by making special efforts to work with minority parents, especially those for whom English is not their native language, on improving their children's learning in science.

Precautions and Possible Pitfalls

Teachers should make sure that multicultural aspects of lessons are not done in a patronizing manner. Also, they should try to be broad in their multicultural focus so that no particular cultural group (e.g., African American, Latino, Asian) feels it is being left out.

Sources

Banks, J. A. (1994). Transforming the mainstream curriculum. *Educational Leadership, 51*(8), 4-8.

Bishop, A. (1988). Mathematics education in its cultural context. *Educational Studies in Mathematics, 19*, 179-191.

Gallard, A. J. (1992). Creating a multicultural learning environment in science classrooms. *Research Matters to the Science Teacher, NARST News, 34*(14), 1-9.

Mendez, P. (1989). *The black snowman.* New York: Scholastic.

Moses, R., Kamii, M., Swap, S., & Howard, J. (1989). The Algebra Project: Organizing in the spirit of Ella. *Harvard Educational Review, 59*(4), 423-443.

Pugh, S. (1990). Introducing multicultural science teaching to a secondary school. *Secondary Science Review, 71*(256), 131-135.

Strutchens, M. (1995). *Multicultural mathematics: A more inclusive mathematics.* ERIC Digest. Clearinghouse for Science, Mathematics and Environmental Education, Columbus, OH.

Strategy 58: Confront your own ethnic and cultural student stereotypes. That will help you develop strategies for creating a more multiculturally sensitive pedagogy.

What the Research Says

The introduction to Tyrone Howard's (2001) research paper describes a range of published research projects that consistently document the consequences of multicultural insensitivity by teachers from the student perspective. The consequences range from passive and active educational resistance as a form of disapproval to nonengagement, cheating, and disruption of class or withdrawing quietly as a way of coping.

Howard's research examined the historical range of research that attempted to gauge the loudness of a multicultural student's voice in the educational equation all stakeholders share. Howard found that culturally relevant pedagogy recognized the cogent role that cultural socialization plays in how students receive, analyze, and interpret information. Culturally sensitive teaching and learning must go well beyond content modification. Modifying content does little to change how students perceive and respond to a noncaring environment.

Howard's study examined student perceptions and interpretations of instructional practices used by four elementary school teachers in four urban settings who were identified as culturally responsive teachers for African American students. A total of 17 students were used in the study. Data were collected through observations and interviews with students. The purposes of student interviews focused on two areas. The first was to gain insight into viewpoints of ethnically diverse students that are rarely revealed in research about teaching and learning. The second was to balance the perceptions and interpretations of teaching practices between the student's viewpoint, the observer's viewpoint, and the teacher's intended goals and objectives.

Results indicate that culturally relevant teaching and learning should focus equally or more on how students are taught rather than what students are taught.

Classroom Applications

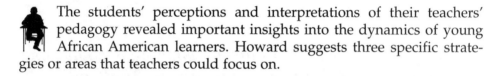 The students' perceptions and interpretations of their teachers' pedagogy revealed important insights into the dynamics of young African American learners. Howard suggests three specific strategies or areas that teachers could focus on.

- **Caring:** Explicit and implicit showing of sincere concern and care that teachers have for their students is vital. Positive reinforcement, expression of high expectations, and taking the time to find out about students' lives outside the classroom are vital to ethnic and cultural sensitivity. The commitment to both the academic and social development of students is the most important expression of concern and care.

- **Establishing community:** The students in this study mentioned on repeated occasions their fondness for family or community-like environments in their classrooms by encouraging kindred relationships in academic settings, the elimination of homogeneous ability groupings (both formal and informal), establishing appropriate democratic principles, and the promotion of interdependence.

- **Engaging classroom environments:** Creating exciting and stimulating classroom environments is not a new idea, but this goes beyond the physical environment and focuses on the style of discourse. Connecting course content to the students' lives and modifying the style of discourse in ways that are more interactive, engaging, and entertaining for students are suggested.

Surprisingly, the study found that no students mentioned teacher race or ethnicity. The job for teachers is to acquire an understanding of the various cultural and learning characteristics their students bring to the classroom. Teachers who want to acquire an authentic understanding of the cultural aura students possess need, among other things, to abandon deficit-based stereotypes about the cognitive capacity, sociocultural backgrounds, and overall learning potential different ethnic groups bring to the classroom. There must be a willingness to make changes to pedagogy to align more with the students' way of knowing, communicating, and being. Far too often ethnic groups are asked or expected to leave their cultural identities at the door and conform to the teachers' way of thinking.

To make all this happen, teachers need to realize that this type of knowledge comes not only from books, but more important from parents, students, and community members. This may mean that teachers should immerse themselves in the day-to-day environment that the students experience. For new teachers, a strong will and courage may be their most needed asset.

Precautions and Possible Pitfalls

When developing effective teacher-student relationships, it is often difficult for new teachers to create clear, workable boundaries between the roles that all teachers have to play in dealing with students. Enabling questionable behavior in the quest for acceptance can create huge discipline and management problems. In the long run, setting reasonable and high standards for behavior, discourse, and pedagogy will establish a teacher's reputation as fair and culturally sensitive. By the time the second and third year of teaching roll around, teachers' reputations will help alleviate misunderstandings about their role and teaching style, and any expectations for the class before students enter the room. Finding a comfort zone in how a teacher deals with students takes time and is always considered work in progress. A teacher should look at establishing a three-year plan and should try not to ignore the challenges students present or find quick-fix solutions, which usually means trying to adopt another teacher's system. Rather the teacher should be reflective, examine personal core philosophies, and adjust them for more long-term solutions. A teacher should see good teaching more as a journey than a destination.

Source

Howard, T. C. (2001). Telling their side of the story: African-American students' perceptions of culturally relevant teaching. *Urban Review, 33*(2), 131-149.

Strategy 59: Welcome and embrace the diversity of today's classrooms.

What the Research Says

That today's schools are more diverse than ever is undeniable. According to the Federal Interagency Forum on Child and Family Statistics (1998), one in every three students currently attending primary or secondary schools today is of a racial or ethnic minority. Predictions are also that students of color will make up almost 50% of the U.S. school-age population by 2020 (Banks & Banks, 2001). With the large influx of immigrants in the past several decades, children of these immigrants make up approximately 20% of the children in the United States, providing a kaleidoscope of cultural and language differences in many classrooms (Dugger, 1998).

Cultural and language differences are only a part of the diversity in our schools. One in five children under the age of 18 currently lives below the poverty line. The traditional two-parent family is becoming the minority. Less than half of America's children currently live with both biological parents, with almost 60% of all students living in a single-parent household by the time they reach the age of 18 (Salend, 2001). All this is occurring at a time when schools are working toward mainstreaming and the inclusion of nearly 11% of school-age children who are classified as disabled (U.S. Department of Education, 1995). Certainly the challenges that face today's classrooms have never been greater. Teacher preparation programs are including classes to help prepare future teachers for cross-cultural, inclusive instruction. Zeichner (1993) proposed that the key characteristics of these programs provide for the dynamics of prejudice and racism.

Classroom Applications

Even in today's society some classrooms seem to be focusing on the differences and difficulties involved in multicultural education, rather than embracing these differences as being enriching, desirable, inevitable, natural, and welcomed. Teachers must not only acknowledge the obvious diversity issues such as color and physical disability, but also be aware of the cultural diversity of students and families. In selecting curriculum it is important to see if examples of diversity are represented. Are the visual examples only of Caucasians? Are the holidays represented in literature only those celebrated by Christians? Are the needs and emotions of the handicapped presented? When having a discussion of families, it is important to stress that not all family units are alike. When sending a note home to parents, it is better to have it addressed to the "parent or guardian of" instead of "mother" or "father." A teacher once asked her students to describe their bedrooms and draw pictures of them. What this teacher didn't realize was that several students did not have their own bedrooms but shared the room with four or five other siblings. Disclosing this information to the class by reading their story and showing their drawings might have been embarrassing for these students. By the same token, new teachers must be especially aware of district and state education codes with regard to celebrating religious holidays in the classroom. What about the student who doesn't celebrate Christian or Jewish holidays? Rather than asking students to write a story about their favorite Christmas memory, the teacher might assign students to write about a favorite family tradition. One question a teacher should consider is "could this question, example, or assignment, make a student feel uncomfortable with regard to their race, religion, ethnic, or cultural background?" Designing a richly diverse curriculum does not have to be difficult; it simply takes thought and consideration. The use of cooperative learning groups lends itself particularly well to teaching students with differing abilities in the same classroom. Students should be grouped with consideration to differences in gender, race, ethnicity, and ability. Using assignments and activities that incorporate the recognition of multiple intelligences is particularly necessary and effective in responding to student diversity.

Precautions and Possible Pitfalls

Frequently it is beginning teachers who find themselves with the most diverse classroom. It is of the utmost importance that these teachers are prepared for cross-cultural, inclusive instruction. Classes in teacher education programs must include information about the characteristics of prejudice and racism, provide successful examples of teaching ethnic- and language-minority students, and ingrain instruction that provides both social support for students and an intellectual challenge.

Teachers must also be sensitive to issues involving money. Perhaps every child in class wouldn't be able to afford the cost of a field trip. For one high school that was considering putting ATM machines on campus, the realization of the ways this could further divide students into "haves" and "have-nots" caused administrators to rethink their decision.

Teachers should consult with experienced exemplary veteran teachers or school administrators before meeting with parents of immigrant students to determine if a translator might be needed or if there is any specific information about that student's family culture which might assist the teacher in having a successful meeting. The same is true for a student with disabilities. The special education teacher and the IEP (individual education program) can provide beneficial information to the novice teacher. The more a teacher is sensitive to the richness of the diversity in the classroom, the more successful and equitable today's classrooms will become.

Sources

Banks, J. A., & Banks, C.A. M. (2001). *Multicultural education: Issues and perspectives* (4th ed.). New York: John Wiley & Sons.

Dugger, C. W. (1998, March 21). Among young of immigrants, outlook rises. *New York Times*, A1, A11.

Federal Interagency Forum on Child and Family Statistics. (1998). *America's children: Key national indicators of well-being*. Washington, DC: U.S. Government Printing Office.

Salend, S. J. (2001). *Creating inclusive classrooms: Effective and reflective practices* (4th ed.). Upper Saddle River, NJ: Merrill.

U.S. Department of Education. (1995). *17th annual report to Congress on the implementation of IDEA*. Washington, DC: Author.

Zeichner, K. M. (1993). *Educating teachers for diversity*. East Lansing, MI: National Center for Research on Teacher Learning.

Strategy 60: Be sensitive to issues affecting gay and lesbian youth.

What the Research Says

Several research studies suggest that approximately one in ten of the students served by public schools will develop gay and lesbian identities before graduation (Cook, 1991; Gonsiorek, 1988). Sexual orientation, however, appears to be established prior to adolescence, perhaps from conception, and is not subject to change (Gonsiorek, 1988; Savin-Williams, 1990).

The social stigma surrounding homosexuality discourages many gay and lesbian teens from discussing the confusion and turmoil they may feel about their emerging identities (Friend, 1993). Add to this sense of confusion the isolation they may feel, and it should not come as a surprise that gay and lesbian youth are "two to six times more likely" than heterosexual teens to attempt suicide. While gay and lesbian teens account for 30% of all completed suicides among adolescents, they comprise only 10% of the teen population (Cook, 1991).

Classroom Applications

Gay and lesbian youth face many of the same changes with regard to social, biological, and cognitive development as their heterosexual counterparts. However, the misconceptions and stigmas, combined with the homophobic cultural climate of our society, often add to the stress and turmoil that many of our gay and lesbian youth struggle with on a daily basis.

Adolescence is a difficult time at best, and these years can be hell on earth for students struggling with issues relating to their sexual orientation. Students can be very cruel to each other and this seems to be heightened more so during adolescence. The physical and emotional safety of every student in class should be paramount. Teachers of middle and high school students can do a lot to provide a safe and harassment-free environment. Not allowing derogatory words or comments in class is a start. If a teacher does not address these negative comments, the gay or lesbian student can further feel alienated and alone. Silence from the teacher is interpreted many times as agreement with what is being said. Because homosexuality appears to be one of the last bastions of "acceptable" discrimination, our gay and lesbian youth may feel more isolated and withdrawn than our heterosexual students. These perceptions of inferiority can lead to poor self-esteem, substance abuse, sexual promiscuity with the opposite sex (to "conceal" their true feelings), and possibly suicide. Teachers would not tolerate students calling each other by racial, ethnic, or religious slurs; therefore we must not tolerate comments of a negative nature to our gay and lesbian students either.

It is up to each and every teacher to provide a safe, nurturing, and respectful environment for every student.

Precautions and Possible Pitfalls

Just because a teacher doesn't have a student (or students) coming out to him or her doesn't mean that teacher doesn't have any gay or lesbian students in the classroom. Given many research studies which estimate one in ten persons are homosexual, it stands to reason that in a class of 30 students a teacher might have three who are struggling with sexual orientation issues. Don't assume that if no one is coming forward to complain about harassment or name calling that the "problem" doesn't exist.

Students may pose questions to the teacher about homosexuality (is it OK, why are some people heterosexual and some people homosexual, etc.). It is not advisable to get into a discussion of right and wrong, OK or not OK. However, telling students that *every* person is entitled to respect, acknowledgement, and acceptance is not only OK, it is the right thing to do.

Sources

Cook, A. T. (1991). Who is killing whom? Issue Paper 1. (Available from Respect All Youth Project, Federation of Parents and Friends of Lesbians and Gays, P.O. Box 27605, Washington, DC 20038.)

Friend, R. A. (1993). Choices, not closets: Heterosexism and homophobia in schools. In L. Weis & M. Fine (Eds.), *Beyond silenced voices: Class, race, and gender in United States schools* (pp. 209-235). Albany: State University of New York.

Gonsiorek, J. C. (1988). Mental health issues of gay and lesbian adolescents. *Journal of Adolescent Health Care*, 114-122.

Savin-Williams, R. C. (1990). Gay and lesbian adolescents. *Marriage and Family Review, 14*, 197-216.

> ☑ *Strategy 61: Prepare yourself for the specialized requirements of placement in an urban multicultural setting. Do not underestimate the amount of preparation that may be necessary for effective teaching there.*

What the Research Says

 This study (Barry & Lechner, 1995) examined a group of preservice teachers' awareness and attitudes about various aspects of multicultural teaching and learning. The group consisted of 73 students enrolled in undergraduate teaching methods classes at a large university in the southeastern United States. The majority of the subjects were white females. Surveys and questionnaires were primary sources of data.

Results indicated that these education majors were aware of many issues related to multicultural education and anticipated a diverse classroom experience in their future. Most were undecided and had little confidence (60.3%) as to just how well their teacher preparation had developed their abilities to teach children from cultural and religious backgrounds other than their own. This included communication with the students' families. However, 49% felt confident in their ability to locate and evaluate culturally diverse materials. The major recommendations and conclusions focused on education programs and coursework discussing potential changes and alterations to teacher training curricula and pedagogy.

Classroom Applications

 Often people look to colleges and universities for expert opinions on a wide range of topics. Academics make a living creating new knowledge and act as repositories of the most current thinking on many of the major issues of today. However, teachers should not necessarily find security in their ability to train for a multicultural experience. Research suggests that there is a wide range of competency within teacher education programs nationwide.

Most teachers are culture-bound and have little experience looking at life through the eyes of other ethnic and religious cultures and socioeconomic levels. The most common suggestions coming out of the research for teacher candidates or preservice teachers centered on individuals volunteering for service or finding a local, knowledgeable, nonjudgmental mentor in school districts the teachers might apply to. Both suggestions can be arranged in any number of ways, both formally and informally.

The teacher can ask school personnel in the district for suggestions on how best to become prepared. Another suggestion focused on selectively picking faculty in a teacher education program which offers the most realistic help in preparing a teacher for placement in ethnically sensitive settings.

If beginning teachers plan to apply or are considering applying to multicultural urban schools, they can take a proactive role in seeking out the right kind of help before becoming disillusioned because of lack of preparation or naiveté.

Precautions and Possible Pitfalls

There are not too many pitfalls in becoming more proactive in these matters. It is no secret that ill-prepared teachers become very disillusioned about teaching and their career choice. Teaching is hard enough without underestimating the potential rigors a teacher might face in unfamiliar settings.

Source

Barry, N. H., & Lechner, J. V. (1995). Preservice teachers' attitudes and awareness of multicultural teaching and learning. *Teaching and Teacher Education, 11*(2), 149-161.

Strategy 62: Become culturally literate when entering diverse school districts. Prepare yourself for the complexities of unpredictable ethnic behaviors.

What the Research Says

The purpose of this specific study was to examine how ethically encapsulated first-year teachers coped with and responded to black youths' ethnic behavior in a desert southwest school. It is not surprising that the research found that beginning teachers who are not prepared for oppositional ethnic behavior can act in ways that diminish black children's (and we assume children from other ethnic groups) school learning and cultural identity. It was found that when underprepared white teachers confronted oppositional behavior from ethnically mixed environments, their educational techniques acted to increase racial tension and hindered their own development, reduced student achievement, and reduced ethnic sensitivity in the school.

In this research, a case study of a first-year, white male teacher provided multiple sources of data from reflective journaling, interview transcripts, and field observations. Reduced enrollment in his monocultural home community forced the new teacher to seek a teaching position elsewhere. His first school featured demographics with whites being the minority culture. Because of a surplus of teachers, after the fifth week he was transferred to another urban school position within the same district. Four months later, finding he could not cope with the behavior of the mostly black student body, he arranged to be transferred to a high school like the one he attended where he was again part of the majority culture. Management strategies he was most familiar with failed and only increased negative ethnic attitudes. He was not able to develop productive relationships with black students. Ethnic origins, cultural experiences, and beliefs about schooling were issues limiting influences on how this teacher and his black students viewed themselves and each other. The need to establish one's cultural identity (symbolic or otherwise) through behavior brought social consequences that hindered the development of an educational relationship.

Classroom Applications

The findings in this study (Birrell, 1995) suggest that principals in multicultural or multiethnic schools should know something about the racial attitudes of the teachers they hire. Most new teachers just want to find work, and their child-centered perspectives provide them with a false sense of security in dealing with multicultural settings. Their positive attitudes can become very short-lived. Beginning teacher demographics tell us that the majority of these teachers have had few opportunities to explore racial attitudes during preservice programs. They typically have limited experience in minority cultures before entering their first classroom.

If teachers find themselves in this position, they should not underestimate the rigors and potential consequences of the situation. They might consider seeking out skilled mentors to help them cope with the acclimation to unfamiliar territory. A culturally sensitive mentor could help new teachers explore their own feelings and help them reflect on the assignment. Beginning teachers should do what they have to do to find the help needed. There are no rules on where to find this help. Principals may be able to suggest someone on site or within a local university education department, or teachers might expand their search to other departments where culture and ethnic sensitivity is important and there are knowledgeable people willing and able to help.

Precautions and Possible Pitfalls

For many good reasons teachers may find they are indeed better suited for classrooms like those that the new teacher in the study experienced. A teacher may also be better or best prepared to teach in that setting. See this as an option. However, if a person is a good teacher, teaching in an upper-middle-class suburban school will do little to help reverse the social, political, economic, and educational factors that perpetuate the multicultural divide.

Sources

Birrell, J. R. (1995). "Learning how the game is played": An ethnically encapsulated beginning teacher's struggle to prepare black youth for a white world. *Teaching and Teacher Education, 11*(2), 137-147.

Burant, T. J. (1999). Finding, using, and losing voice: A preservice teacher's experiences in an urban educational practicum. *Journal of Teacher Education, 50*(3), 209.

Terrill, M. M., & Mark, D. (2000). Preservice teachers' expectations for schools with children of color and second-language learners. *Journal of Teacher Education, 51*(2), 149.

Strategy 63: Eliminate signs of subtle gender bias in your classroom discourse.

What the Research Says

Many observational studies demonstrate that male students participate more in class than female students and that teacher behaviors contribute to this pattern (Baily, 1988; Biklen & Pollard, 1993; Sadker & Sadker, 1986; Sadker, Sadker & Steindam, 1989). Typical patterns found that

- Male students receive more attention and more specific feedback from teachers.
- Males are more likely to receive praise for the intellectual content of their answers.
- Teachers rarely wait more than five seconds for a response to questions and rarely call on nonvolunteers. This type of discourse favors aggressive male students.
- Many teachers are unaware of their own discriminatory behaviors until someone calls it to their attention.
- Gender equity is rarely a component of teacher education programs.
- Teachers have a misconception that they are not responsible for bias in the classroom and the students are. If teachers believe that students, not teachers, are to blame for gender bias, it will continue.
- Prospective teachers' beliefs may interfere with current concepts and ideas in gender-bias components of teacher education.

In this study 48 preservice teachers (21 male, 27 female) were involved in trying to answer the following questions:

1. How do preservice teachers' perceptions of gender interactions compare with actual gender interaction data?

2. Do prospective teachers become aware of the limits of their own perceptions in detecting inequities in classroom interaction?

3. What strategies do preservice teachers propose to ensure equity?

4. Do preservice teachers report changing any beliefs about subtle gender bias?

These preservice teachers were all enrolled in sections of an educational psychology class. Gender interaction patterns were recorded and researched using a variety of techniques both in their classes and during outside field experience. Some of the highlights of their results included the following:

- 73% said they would promote equity and make a conscious effort to ensure equity in seating, lab work, cooperative groups, and athletic activities, and ensure equity in curriculum content and language use.
- 24% said they would collect data to become aware of or to monitor gender bias (videotape, outside observers).
- 21% said they would become more aware of seating arrangements and pairing of males and females.
- 18% said they would balance guest speakers and gender bias in curriculum.
- Several planned to use inclusive language to switch gender roles for demonstrations, clean-up, and so on.
- 35% of the students reported changes of conformations of their beliefs about gender equity.

In discussions, it was felt that interventions of this sort in teacher education programs increased awareness of gender bias. The majority of students discussed the need to collect data and monitor classroom interaction in order to ensure equity in their future classrooms.

The answer to question four seemed to be beyond the scope of the study.

Classroom Applications

 There are two categories of action that teachers can take from this research.

1. Believe that gender bias exists and, just like preparing other components of pedagogy, keep gender bias as a highly considered element. View existing research on the subject and adjust teaching style where it is needed.

2. Informal action research can alert teachers to subtle biases they may not be aware of. Videotape a teacher's interactions or have someone observe a teacher's teaching. It doesn't need to be publishable, only personally reflective of the teacher's classroom discourse. Make appropriate changes to instructional strategies and classroom discourse.

Most of the students in the study believe that if they had not experienced gender bias, it was because they were not really aware of it. Once becoming aware of the fine details of gender bias in the classroom, the project showed them that their perception might not fit reality.

Precautions and Possible Pitfalls

⚠️ Boys and girls have acquired their behaviors and roles over time. They need to be taught how to recognize gender bias in their own lives. There are many students that are so comfortable in their roles that they would resist changing. Teachers should consider keeping their equity goals as part of a hidden or subtle curriculum. Students acquired their roles over a long time and from many places, and teachers should keep their expectations reasonable. They may not see the desired changes in the short time they work with the students.

Sources

Baily, G. D. (1988). Identifying sex equitable interaction patterns in classroom supervision. *NASSP Bulletin, 72*, 95-98.

Biklen, S. K., & Pollard, D. (1993). *Gender and education. Ninety-second yearbook of the national society for the study of education (part 1)*. Chicago: University of Chicago Press.

Lundeberg, M. A. (1997). You guys are overreacting: teaching prospective teachers about subtle gender bias. *Journal of Teacher Education, 48*, (1), 55.

Sadker, M., & Sadker, D. (1994). *Failing at fairness: how America's schools cheat girls*. New York: Charles Scribner's Sons.

Sadker, M., & Sadker, D. (1986, Fall). Equity and excellence: A contradiction in terms? *Theory Into Practice*.

Sadker, M., Sadker, D., & Steindam, S. (1989). Gender equity and educational reform. *Educational Leadership, 46*(6), 44-47.

Strategy 64: View yourself through the eyes of your students. How students view successful teachers differs for girls and boys.

What the Research Says

📚 Girls are more critical of a teacher's appearance and behavior than boys. Female teachers were evaluated more frequently than male teachers as unfair and too soft. However, female teachers were regarded as less nervous, less disorderly, and are more punctual than male teachers. Female teachers do not make excessive demands on students and they smoke less. Female teachers get thoroughly evaluated by students in terms of their social behavior and their dress. Male teachers were evaluated more critically in terms of their politics and philosophy. Participants were 40 male and female teachers and their students from Grades 5 to 10. The experiment consisted of four phases:

- Phase 1: Questionnaire that asked students for their view of the characteristics of effective teachers
- Phase 2: Observation of teachers' actions during lessons
- Phase 3: Analyses of teachers' personalities
- Phase 4: Procedures to improve or stabilize favorable teacher characteristics

The results showed that cheerfulness was the characteristic that was named by students of all age groups. Most student views of the characteristics of effective teachers changed with the students' age. For example, being good at explaining facts was considered an effective characteristic by 34% of eighth graders, 41% of ninth graders, and 50% of tenth graders. The most frequent negative characteristics identified were being nervous, making excessive demands, being disorderly, being late, and smoking. Thirteen positive characteristics of effective teachers were identified:

1. Having good methodology

2. Identifying the aim of a lesson

3. Dividing tasks into parts

4. Supplying or demanding summaries of a lesson

5. Giving tasks with a high degree of difficulty

6. Getting students to think automatically

7. Not making intimidating comments

8. Involving students actively in learning

9. Not making discouraging comments when students make mistakes

10. Focusing on the essential points

11. Giving students individual help or making individual demands

12. Giving varied assessments

13. Evaluating a student's personality from a positive perspective

Classroom Applications

Teachers should be aware of the characteristics their students attend to. Female teachers are likely to find it harder to get students' respect than male teachers. Since cheerfulness was considered important by students of all ages, teachers could benefit from making a deliberate attempt to be more cheerful, if they are not cheerful already.

Precautions and Possible Pitfalls

⚠️ Being polite, always speaking gently to the students, encouraging them, and so on are things that students expect from female teachers, but this alone does not work. A male teacher should not rely only on his professional knowledge. Although professional knowledge is important, there are other aspects of conducting a lesson that are important.

Source

Grassel, H. (1968). *Probleme und Ergebnisse von Untersuchungen der Lehrertätigkeit und Lehrerwirksamkeit* [*Problems and results of investigations regarding teacher's activity and teacher's effectiveness*]. Rostock: Studie des Wissenschaftsbereichs Pädagogische Psychologie der Universität Rostock.

Strategy 65: Understand that immersion experience can be the best teacher. It can be a multicultural learning opportunity for you and can help prepare you for placement in a multicultural environment.

What the Research Says

Personal background is recognized as an important element in the development and formation of multicultural perspectives in preservice teachers. These previous experiences and backgrounds influence what is taught, the teacher's interpretations of classroom situations, student behaviors, and many instructional decisions. The main background elements of this perspective are outlined here (Smith, 2000):

1. Race, gender, and social membership

2. Prior experience with diversity

3. Support of ideologies of individualism

Two related studies looked at issues related to the following:

- How do the background experiences of preservice teachers influence inclusion of a multicultural perspective in teaching?

- How do preservice teachers' background experiences influence the effectiveness of a teacher education program in achieving multicultural education?
- How could a multicultural immersion program alter their perspectives?

One study examined two preservice teachers, one with limited multicultural experiences and background and another with multicultural experiences. Both were white, with one mainly isolated in her socioeconomic and cultural upbringing and the other immersed in and forced to fit into and adapt to other cultures in other countries. Both taught history in schools of roughly the same size. One teacher's school was slightly more diverse. Overall, the data, from observation, teacher reflection, and student responses, suggest noticeable differences in the two teachers' effectiveness as multicultural teachers. Background experiences and three specific factors—preservice teacher's race, gender, and social class; prior experiences with diversity; and support for ideologies of individualism—would appear to offer a partial explanation for these differences. While the two subjects seemed to be at opposite and extreme ends of the multicultural spectrum, the researchers felt there were valid concerns their work could bring to education programs regarding how background experiences influence

- Sensitivity and cultural congruence
- Knowledge of students' background
- Awareness of learning styles
- Recognition of racism, classism, and sexism
- A high school student's perception of the teacher's teaching

This case study, while it included only two teachers, did provide tentative support for the explanatory power of background in a teacher's ability to respond to multicultural pedagogy. Important questions that the study did not answer were

- What experiences or strategies appear to be successful in expanding a preservice teacher's multicultural literacy?
- Is it possible to broaden the experiences and beliefs of all preservice teachers, and should multicultural experiences be a prerequisite for admission to a teacher education program?

The results of this study clearly found a connection between multicultural background and a teacher's ability to deal with multicultural settings. However, the researchers did recommend further studies using larger sample sizes and a wider range of research questions.

The other study examined how a very short-term immersion in a multicultural setting affected a group of student teachers or teachers within a teacher preparation program. Three classes of 86 students in their fifth year of a five-year education program were asked to immerse themselves in an unfamiliar multicultural experience of their choice and respond with project write-ups. Settings ranged from African Americans in church to gay bars and Quaker meetings. Students had to take the initiative in their self-growth by arranging their cultural immersion experience themselves. Most students were reported as being displeased with the project and expressed discomfort and anxiety. Afterward, they overwhelmingly endorsed the project as valuable and memorable and stated it was the most important course assignment. However, the experience did have a neutral effect on a few, and some made little effort to fully engage and immerse themselves. Some expressed a feeling of guilt about infiltrating a group without explaining why they were there. Others were resistant to the situation they entered, and this compromised the effectiveness of the experience.

Judging from the feedback, the researcher felt that the project had a meaningful effect on the students but made no claims about the lasting or cumulated effect of other multicultural activities.

Classroom Applications

The research speaks to experience as the best teacher in preparation for a multicultural placement. Classroom discussions and activities can only go so far in their contribution to a new teacher's range of multicultural insight and tactics. The first study, while narrow in scope, pointed to previous experience in multiethnic and multicultural settings as important in developing positive teaching attributes. The second study placed education majors in multicultural noneducational settings with documented positive short-term results. Most of this should come as no surprise. If one is new to the teaching pool, there is a good chance a teacher's first job may be in an unfamiliar social, cultural, or ethnic environment. These studies point out a need for new teachers to fill in the multicultural gaps in their training.

Beginning teachers may not want to trust their teacher education program to do the job. Remember that getting a teaching job is only the beginning. The new teacher will be working toward keeping the job. More important, the teachers may want to personally feel effective and in control of any situation they are asked to tackle. The more a teacher experiences the conditions and the more understanding and knowledge one brings to the job, the more comfortable the teacher will feel. Suggestions include some of the following activities:

- Volunteer for placement in settings you are not familiar with.
- Scout out the communities to which you will be applying ahead of time.

- Reflect on your own fears and limits. What conditions can you overcome with preparation and which should you avoid?
- Find support in community groups and colleagues in your preparation.
- Research and read the professional literature.
- Look for colleges and universities that offer proven and effective preparation. Go back to school if necessary or seek professional inservices and workshops.

Research indicates that experience beats outs classwork most of the time when preparing for multicultural settings.

Precautions and Possible Pitfalls

 There don't seem to be many pitfalls here. Preparation for a multicultural setting is very individualized, and each new or potential teacher needs to be honest and very proactive. One program can't meet the requirements of all participants. Individuals, based on their unique needs and goals, may have to go well beyond the program to fill in holes in their preparation. One large pitfall would be to underestimate the challenges a multicultural classroom of kids, their parents, and the community can present.

Sources

Smith, R. W. (2000). The influence of teacher background on the inclusion of multicultural education: a case study of two contrasts. *Urban Review*, *32*(2), 155-176.

Wiest, L. R. (1998). Using immersion experiences to shake up preservice teacher views about cultural differences. *Journal of Teacher Education*, *49*(5), 358-365.

 Strategy 66: Prepare for a cultural and linguistic mismatch between you and your students.

What the Research Says

The majority of future teachers in the United States are white, monolingual, and female (Cushner, McClelland, & Safford, 1996). In contrast, their students will increasingly be of diverse cultures and will be second-language learners (Hodgkinson, 1985; Pallas, Natriello, & McDill, 1989).

Due to this potential mismatch, future teachers will be called upon to teach in classrooms and to students very different from their own cultural background. As a group, these new teachers will generally come from rural colleges and universities and will find their first assignments teaching in urban classrooms populated with second-language learners. They will bring a certain cultural, racial, linguistic, and economic background and expectations for urban life. These expectations will not likely be based on firsthand experiences. Here are some questions the researchers thought a teacher should consider:

- How does the experiential background affect how these teachers approach the urban experience?
- What expectations do they have for urban students and communities, and how does this affect their planning as they prepare curricular materials for gifted and talented and at the same time for curricular remediation?
- Do their management plans and strategies indicate they expect most of their students to be behaved and naturally motivated or difficult and unmotivated?
- Will they feel comfortable with parent and community contacts and home visits or will they avoid communication and after-school activities because they feel unsafe in the community?

Various studies (Terrill & Mark, 2000) point to future teachers exhibiting negative attitudes and perceptions toward urban schools and minority learners. They point out that most people tend to be culture-bound, and teachers with no experience in the backgrounds of their students are limited in their ability to interact effectively and professionally. They are not ready to shape cultural partnerships and teach in culturally diverse classrooms. These studies also found that preservice and student teachers' personal experiences during childhood and adolescence were the major determinants of their cultural perspectives, and most had little experience in diverse cultural settings.

Classroom Applications

Teachers can look upon the potential problems presented by the research as their own or pass them off as a problem for the teacher education institutions. Teachers may think they are getting that job in their first school of choice, but are the teachers prepared to move on if they don't? What if a teacher's institution of higher education doesn't include a heavy dose of multicultural education throughout their curriculum?

Will the teacher be prepared? The reality is teachers and their classmates will be competing for jobs in very diverse settings. The demographics point out that it is very likely new teachers will be working in cultural demographics very different from their own. It is up to the individual teachers to squeeze out every bit of help they can find within their program to become prepared. Teachers should seek out the professors that seem to be more in tune to multicultural themes and training. The new teacher will then be better prepared to bridge potential cultural and linguistic gaps.

Next, consider service-learning opportunities in diverse settings. These experiences will increase levels of comfort and reduce anxiety. Teachers should be prepared to confront their cultural and linguistic assumptions, perceptions, and expectations. They will be able to help students with an expanded awareness and have a more inclusive, tolerant, and larger knowledge base.

Finally, new teachers should consider developing strategies to explore their own cultural, linguistic, and racial identities and biases. Teachers will find it is hard to explore and appreciate the worldviews of others without a grasp of their own. As a new teacher it is important to develop a knowledge base of the major paradigms and concepts of multicultural education, diverse cultures, and ethnic and social groups. Schools don't want educators who are afraid of their communities, expect the worst in the classroom, and rarely see their students as gifted and talented and being motivated.

Precautions and Possible Pitfalls

New teachers shouldn't assume their own subject matter or content mastery is the most important factor in preparation for the classroom. Depending on the settings teachers find themselves in, management and people skills will make a job much easier. Multicultural educational settings require diverse teaching tools. One size doesn't fit all, and teachers will need to provide multiple learning pathways in the same class. Many students and classroom demographics will exhibit needs well beyond the curriculum content.

As the teacher prepares for the classroom and with the help of supervising professors and master teachers, there is a need to become aware of and focus on some of those intangible areas beyond the content that diverse learners present.

Sources

Cushner, K., McClelland, A., & Safford, P. (1996). *Human diversity in education: An integrative approach*. New York: McGraw-Hill.

Hodgkinson, H. (1985). *All one system: Demographics of education, kindergarten through graduate school* (ED 261 101). Washington DC: Institute for Educational Leadership.

Pallas, A. M., Natriello, G., & McDill, E. L. (1989). The changing nature of disadvantaged population: current dimensions and future trends. *Educational Research, 18*(5), 16-22.

Terrill, M. M., & Mark, D. (2000). Preservice teachers' expectations for schools with children of color and second-language learners. *Journal of Teacher Education, 51*(2), 149.

Strategy 67: Develop gender literacy, as students do come with gender biases. Be aware that students (especially male students) sometimes treat female teachers different from how they treat male teachers.

What the Research Says

The researcher interviewed 16 women from three teacher education programs in New England to learn about their experiences as female student teachers and acquired insight into the gender issues in female student teachers' lives. More than half the women interviewed spoke of being demeaned and objectified. One of the most evident gender issues coming from the study was male high school students' harassment of female student teachers. They told stories of how the cultural habit of viewing women as sex objects affected the environment in which they began teaching.

An in-depth interviewing technique was used to gather information related to specific incidents and how these related to their lives and what it was like as a woman to student teach. The predominant complaint centered on how male students feel entitled to exert power in a school context and demean and dehumanize female student teachers through objectification. Other male students are often mute or provide open support to these behaviors.

Their behaviors are described as a power struggle between genders. Male students, who, especially in secondary schools, are relegated to lower power relationships, grab control by transforming the recognized authority in the room to a powerless object of their discourse. Language becomes their weapon.

Classroom Applications

Teacher educators and the teachers themselves must develop ways to first become aware of gender issues embedded in management, curricular, and discipline issues and then become more cognizant of the gender factors within their context. Many can arise from deeply rooted sexist attitudes both within the teachers themselves and within their students.

There are culture-driven gender issues that female teachers must confront in their own thinking. The study pointed to a critical juncture during the middle school years in which girls either learn to be honest about what they see and know around them or deny what they see and know. The researchers found when the girls confront individuals or institutions in their lives, they risk losing relationships with parents, teachers, and friends. If they remain silent, they are more likely to maintain peaceful relationships with these same people. Most girls choose silence. When these women make the transition from student to teacher, from dependence to independence, from passive to active initiator, they need a reservoir of support to draw from. There is a residue from growing up female in the U.S. culture, and this residue can show up again at this vulnerable time of learning to teach.

Another problem lies within potential supporting collaborators. Not everyone in the support context may possess enough insight, experience, or empathy to help. Not everyone has the insight to recognize potential gender issues.

Precautions and Possible Pitfalls

Teachers should not overreact and make every sexist remark, look, or comment their own problem. A teacher should pick the battles carefully and tread lightly as some of these entrenched attitudes are invisible to the students themselves. In all likelihood each incident will need to be treated differently, and a different strategy will be needed.

Source

Miller, J. H. (1997). Gender issues embedded in the experience of student teaching: Being treated like a sex object. *Journal of Teacher Education, 48*(1), 19-28.

8

Integrating Technology in the Classroom

 Strategy 68: Balance the rigors of new technology with content goals. When helping students acquire computer and technology skills, teach them to set goals that focus on the process of learning instead of on the product or outcome of learning.

What the Research Says

It's beneficial to teach students to set learning goals for different reasons, and different kinds of goals have different effects. Goal setting can affect students' achievement and motivation, and it can affect how students regulate the use of their thoughts, actions, and feelings. Students can use the goals they set as standards for assessing their own progress. Goals focusing on the learning process emphasize the strategies that students use in acquiring skills or information. In contrast, goals focusing on the product of learning emphasize outcomes or results such as how much was accomplished and how long it took. Research conducted on goal setting when teaching students to use the computer indicates that students who set process goals felt that they learned more effectively than students did who set product goals. Students in the process condition believed that they were more competent in performing hypercard tasks (i.e., they had greater self-efficacy) than did students in the product condition, and achievement results showed that process condition students indeed were more successful than students in the product condition in performing hypercard tasks.

Classroom Applications

Have students regularly set process goals when acquiring new knowledge or skills. Use a think-aloud procedure and write on the board to model for students how they should set process goals. Individually or in groups, have students brainstorm process goals they can set for a particular computer task. Require students to write their process goals in their notebooks, and periodically check their notebooks to assess their progress in achieving their goals, looking for new goals to replace those that have already been accomplished. Some process goals may require more time than the product goals. Teachers should not underestimate the rigorous and challenging learning that technology requires to make progress toward a more primary goal or product. The following are some situations that would require sometimes as much or more time learning than actually doing the primary task. Teachers should help students make realistic time estimates including the technology learning curve.

• Student groups needed to learn a spreadsheet and graphing program to be able to manage and summarize the data from a statistics experience. They needed to complete a tutorial and manipulate a few small data sets before looking at their own data.

• Students using a laptop computer with a physiology-sensing capacity needed to learn the accompanying software to make their experiment and data collection fully functional.

• An earth science group accessing a weather and climate Web page was required to learn a Web page's specific programs to manipulate its temperature and rainfall data.

• Students from a high school located near a university needed to master the university library's digital library and e-journal access to acquire the background information for their research paper.

• Students needed to evaluate many curriculum-related Internet sites to assess which sites were the most accurate and useful.

• A graphics program needed to be learned in order to develop overheads and slides to be used in an English presentation.

These are all examples of process goals that may need to be mastered before finishing a project or activity. A teacher shouldn't underestimate the potential techno-process pitfalls and should be patient with students who may have a limited background in technology.

Precautions and Possible Pitfalls

 Teachers should not just let students copy their process goals for learning to use computers or other technology. Self-generated goals are more personally meaningful to students than teacher-imposed goals.

Source

Schunk, D., & Ertmer, P. (1999). Self-regulatory processes during computer skill acquisition: Goal and self-evaluative influences. *Journal of Educational Psychology*, *91*(2), 251-260.

 Strategy 69: Use the Internet as a classroom. The Internet is a source of full and rich inquiry-based curricular alternatives that include not only content but also engaging discipline process opportunities.

What the Research Says

"Kids as Global Scientists" (KGS), characterized as a tele-communication program, is an interactive, integrated, inquiry-based science curriculum project that has been developed by meteorologists and teachers from the University of Michigan and is sponsored by the National Science Foundation. It resides on the Internet, which makes it accessible to large numbers of teachers and students. Its current Internet project engages over 200 schools in interactive investigations. Professional weather experts interact with students, answering their questions. The total length of a unit runs 6 to 8 weeks.

The investigation and interaction is facilitated by the use of specialized interactive software that is designed specifically for the project. The software provides all textbook content and, in addition, connects students to the Internet, simulations, and current imagery collections of weather data and allows them to download data. In one project the program suggests a final project of building a hurricane-safe house and simulating the force of the hurricane by using a leaf blower.

The program provides teacher's guides, software, and all other material needed to empower the project. The program develops thematic units within the earth science discipline of atmospheric science and meteorology.

Research centered on the assessment and evaluation of one class participating in one unit or program. Six sixth-grade students representing three motivational levels were selected for intensive study to help illustrate how different students view learning science and the use of technology both before and after a technology-rich program. Pre- and postassessment scores were analyzed for the entire class, and the six students' comments from individual interviews provided one example of evidence from each motivational level.

Overall, results indicated significant gains in content knowledge and a high level of motivation with the project. Students find the use of the Internet and telecollaborative environments engaging and motivating.

Classroom Applications

This use of the Internet as a classroom is an emerging use of the technology. In addition to the KGS program, there are other such opportunities to engage students in similar programs. Distance learning (type the term in a search engine and you will find a large numbers of sites) is available as an alternative to site-dependent learning. Many colleges and universities and a few high schools now offer participation in digital classrooms. Electronic Advance Placement classes are now offered as alternatives for schools without the ability to provide such programs.

As an inquiry-based science experience, KGS offers an authentic, guided, safe experience that is not only content but also process rich. The use of technological tools provides a motivating vehicle to learn. Not all science works this easily in real life. However, for a taste of real science, this serves the purpose. The Internet educational market is growing. The KGS project is a packaged user-friendly project.

NoodleTools, at www.noodletools.com, is a free suite of interactive tools designed to aid students and professionals with their online research. From selecting a search engine and finding some relevant sources and then citing those sources in MLA style, NoodleTools makes online research easier!

There are a number of Internet sites that act as repositories of data. Climate and weather data are easily available and the GenBank provides almost unlimited genomic and molecular science data. Imaginative, creative, and motivated teachers can develop their own inquiry-based opportunities. Many of these sites offer free data that can be used to answer student questions. The opportunities are open-ended in nature and can be as complex or as simple as the instructor desires. There are even digital libraries that offer access to periodicals and other sources of information. Some access is limited to subscribers, and some sites must be accessed at a college or university that subscribes to the service.

There are too many sites to identify here. At the time of writing this strategy, typing the terms "interactive lessons" in a search engine produced over 5000 hits or sites. Not all these sites are useful, but it does give you the idea there is a lot out there. The interactive nature of some of these sites was found only in software a few years ago. Now it's free.

Precautions and Possible Pitfalls

Although the technology provides a sexy and often motivating alternative to conventional hands-on experiences, the evaluation and preparation time remains the same. It does take time to find and survey the potential that Internet sites offer. Technology has its quirks and breakdowns, and access may not be available on demand or on the class's schedule. Online access can be a problem in some communities.

Appropriate use policies are a necessity, and Web surfing can keep students off-track for extended periods of time. The idea that the Internet can provide serious instruction sometimes requires an adjustment in perception and a context change both with students and with parents.

Source

Mistler-Jackson, M., & Songer, N. (2000). Student motivation and Internet technology: Are students empowered to learn science? *Journal of Research in Science Teaching, 37*(5), 459-479.

Strategy 70: Develop Internet-based literacies. Web-centered curriculum can engage students in the analysis of a diverse range of resources now available on the Internet.

What the Research Says

Bos (2000) recently conducted research to examine the Internet as a source of valid information for science students. The World Wide Web is an exciting and challenging information resource now available to many teachers and students. It is so convenient for students it can become their primary source of information while conducting research for their assignments and projects. The Internet is challenging because of the diverse and often uneven nature of the information presented. This presents both students and teachers with the need to develop new skills of critical analysis and evaluation. Critical evaluation skills have always been an important part of media literacy for students in the context of a science class. Bos's study focused on two aspects of critical evaluation: summarization of science content and evaluation of credibility.

Participants in Bos's study were students in two 11th-grade science sections at an alternative high school in a medium-sized Midwestern college town. The class involved in these studies was in the third year of a "Foundations of Science" sequence, an integrated science curriculum that follows the principles of a project-based approach. It also has a heavy technology component. Forty-four students (27 females and 17 males) took part in the project. The study centered on answering three questions:

1. Can students summarize scientific resources that they find on the Web?

2. Can students identify and evaluate evidence in the scientific resources that they find on the Web?

3. Can students identify the source and potential biases (points of view) of the scientific resources that they find on the Web?

The project produced 63 student Web reviews published by the students. Content analyses showed that student summaries were usually accurate. However, students had problems assessing how comprehensive and detailed sites were. When asked to evaluate credibility, students struggled to identify scientific evidence cited or presented supporting Web site claims. This was a problem because many Web sites do not present evidence as it might be found in a scientific journal format. Students could determine the publishing source but were challenged in identifying potential biases with Web publishers.

The findings of Bos's study can provide teachers with a solid grounding for further development of media literacy activities. Technical and pedagogical scaffolding based on site-specific goals and demands facilitates students acquiring or reinforcing critical evaluation skills.

Classroom Applications

This research has clear implications for science teachers. Many teachers in the sciences present students with opportunities to critically review the validity of science information, content, and its resources as a normal part of scientific thinking. With easy access, the Internet is rapidly becoming students' primary source of information

---

Box 8.1

---

1. Content

What is the purpose of this resource? Who is the target audience?
What scientific claims are made? What information and content are
  available here?

2. Source Credibility

Who is publishing this page? Are there any potential biases or
  conflicts of interest?
How much support or evidence exists for the claims made within the
  resource? Is it referenced or academically cited to back up the
  claims or information beyond common knowledge?

3. Overall Organization

How well organized is the information? Is there a central page where
  everything is accessible? Are there links to other relevant Internet
  sites? How technical is the information?

4. Appearance

Is it a professionally designed resource? Do the graphics support the
  information and help communicate it? Does the resource "teach"
  the information?

---

beyond the textbook for many curricular activities. Therefore, acquiring
Internet-critical evaluation skills will become crucial in developing overall
media literacy.

There are many ways to embed critical evaluation into projects or as a
separate independent activity. Ideally experienced students will be able to
critique Web site information routinely. However, to get to that point, a
teacher may need to begin by creating prompts or triggers to serve as
review categories. This could be as detailed and complex as needed for
beginning student researchers. A simple prompt worksheet might look
like Box 8.1.

Again, the level of guidance, triggers, and prompts can be adjusted to
the class and the experience of the students.

Precautions and Possible Pitfalls

At its best, the Internet and its resources provide students with
an easily accessible source of valid resources for a variety of
curricular activities. However, it can also be a source of biased
content and misinformation. Web-site text can be copied and pasted into
word processing programs. Some students will over-rely on the Internet
and not use other more traditional resources. Teachers should be careful to

make these points clear to students. Students should be encouraged to plan ahead to use other sources of information.

Source

Bos, N. (2000). High school students' critical evaluation of scientific resources on the World Wide Web. *Journal of Science Education and Technology, 9*(2), 161-173.

 Strategy 71: Learn what the International Society for Technology in Education (ISTE) says about standards and student learning. Use its research, analysis, and communication (RAC) model to integrate these standards into your instruction.

What the Research Says

International standards for technology in education were first established by ISTE in 1993. The standards are for all subject areas and grade levels, for students ages 5-18. Specified as standards for *all* teachers, the first edition had 13 performance indicators. The second edition of the standards (1997) grew to 18 indicators, divided into three categories:

1. Basic computer/technology operations and concepts

2. Personal and professional use of technology

3. Application of technology to instruction

The third edition of the standards, "ISTE National Educational Technology Standards for Teachers," consists of 23 performance indicators that are grouped into six categories:

I. Technology operations and concepts

II. Planning and designing learning environments and experiences

III. Teaching, learning, and curriculum

IV. Assessment and evaluation

V. Productivity and professional practices

VI. Social, ethical, legal, and human issues

Technology is not only here to stay, its influence is exploding exponentially in education and all other aspects of life. Teachers need to integrate it into their instruction now, or their students will be left behind in the future.

The RAC model is an instructional framework for integrating technology into the curriculum through lesson planning and assessment across subjects and grade levels. Research suggests that teachers identified the following benefits of RAC lessons:

1. More student-centered learning

2. Students engage in more critical thinking

3. Material can be integrated across subject areas

4. It is easily incorporated into performance-based classrooms

5. Students are required to apply important skills in a meaningful context

6. It provides opportunities to evaluate students' work

Classroom Applications

To plan the use of technology to meet the national standards for both teachers and students, teachers can visit the ISTE Web site (www.iste.org) and download or view the standards. The Web site also has numerous instructional resources to help teachers integrate technology into their instruction in virtually all grades and subjects. Resources include a database of lessons in which a teacher can search for lesson plans that integrate technology into science teaching, specifying the particular topic and grade level needed. The site also contains resources that have been developed for multidisciplinary units and allows teachers to enter their own lesson plans.

According to the ISTE Web site, the "Multidisciplinary Unit Resources" section includes resource units designed to provide powerful themes around which multidisciplinary learning activities can be built. Each unit addresses the theme with a variety of activities, related technology, and thematically relevant information, tools, and resources. Each activity is designed to address content standards from two or more subject areas while also addressing the National Educational Technology Standards (NETS) for student performance indicators. Units for each grade-range provide developmentally appropriate themes, tools, and resources from which teachers can choose when developing specific learning experiences.

Implementing the RAC model involves the following three phases:

1. *Research.* Students gather information from various resources, not just paper and pencil. For example, they go to various Internet sites to acquire information about specific concepts within your curriculum.

2. *Analysis.* Data analysis depends upon the results of the research. Students must think critically and use the information they gathered. For example, like paper resources, students have to gauge the validity of the information, whether it is the most current, biased, or complete enough for their use.

3. *Communication.* Students prepare products to share their results. For example, students can communicate the new information to a wider audience for critical review and critique.

Precautions and Possible Pitfalls

Teachers should not expect themselves or their students to meet all 23 performance indicator standards the first or second time around. Teachers and their students may need more time and experience to assimilate new information and develop new skills. Teachers can use the standards as longer-term goals and to establish performance criteria for assessment purposes.

Source

Bowens, E. M. (2000). Meeting standards with technology. *Learning and Leading With Technology: Serving Teachers in the Classroom, 27*(8), 6-9, 17. Retrieved from www.iste.org.

Strategy 72: Don't let technology overwhelm subject matter. When adding technological tools and their learning curves to classes, it is necessary to make comparable shifts in other areas of the course requirements.

What the Research Says

A traditional undergraduate physics course on math methods was redesigned to incorporate the use of a computerized algebra program throughout all aspects of the course. The goal of this redesign was to expose beginning students to professional tools currently used by mathematicians and physicists. At the same time a new multimedia physics class sought to integrate math and physics content with other multimedia forms. These two classes served as research laboratories to begin a qualitative case study to first describe the course and then develop an understanding of the effect technology had on instruction and learning in the courses. It was found that the instructors of both courses made rather substantial changes in their courses the second time through based on their early experience.

The research provided an overview of the issues as follows:

• Students resisted the additional process orientation of adding technology as another layer of course requirements. Computers add another layer of process skills to learn.

• Teachers needed to be better prepared and have their own technological act together.

• The advanced workload preparing for such courses is enormous and goes unnoticed by the students. To the students, book content represents the curriculum: a reduced use of books leads to a student perception of a reduction in content and course structure.

• There needs to be a means used for demonstrating the technology and a backup plan in case of problems.

• Clear procedures needed to be developed for students to follow when they encountered problems.

• Whenever students seemed to have strong learning preferences and styles, their expectations about how they "ought to be taught" conflicted with the design of the courses. Expectations need to be described explicitly and explained for possible conflicting expectations. Problematic conflicts in how and why instruction is implemented need to be resolved.

• Instructors somewhat underestimated the basic instruction needed. Teachers were challenged to provide guidance and examples without providing "simple" templates that structure the students' homework with little imagination or editing. Technology used as a professional tool required in-class instruction that modeled real problem-solving modes.

Overall, the research suggested that the necessary transition from traditional instruction to tool-based instruction is dramatic and fraught with difficulty for teachers and students. The researchers found their data far less positive or encouraging than they would have liked. As experienced teachers, as technology users, and as scientists foreseeing drastic changes in the kinds of intellectual skills that students are likely to bring to the professional world, they saw a long developmental road ahead.

Classroom Applications

When movable type was invented and the first books printed, all the formatting, running heads, tables of content, page numbers, indexes, and so on were not included. The "technology" of the book is standardized today. We are all familiar with these book standards and so are the students. When you teach a course from a book, most of the time all involved know what to expect.

Calculators, seen as routine today, required a good deal of time to filter through instructional practices and find a niche. Most teachers today have no problem finding a context in their courses for calculators. There are no such standards yet on the World Wide Web.

As new technology continues to filter into the classroom, first we await better-trained students from below. Second, teachers need to address the concerns listed in the research and accept a rather steep learning curve for implementing technology for themselves and their students. The researchers found a remarkable similarity in problems and pitfalls between these two independent classes using very different technologies. Real-world professional tools impose a rather drastic transition for all stakeholders. Become as informed as you can about the technology, but also be aware of the potential transitional pitfalls you will need to address as a professional educator.

Precautions and Possible Pitfalls

Teachers should not underestimate the amount of work, for both themselves and their students, involved in making technological transitions. Frustrated students can sabotage your best efforts by not authentically engaging in the new type of instruction. Students that would do well in traditional classes need nurturing and assurance when the rules change.

Source

Runge, A., Spiegel, A., Pytlik, L., Dunbar, S., Fuller, R., Sowell, G., & Brooks, D. (1999). Hands-on computer use in science classrooms: The skeptics are still waiting. *Journal of Science Education and Technology, 8*(1), 33-44.

Strategy 73: Consider prior knowledge, as your students may know computer technology better than you do.

What the Research Says

The effectiveness of instructional methods when teaching students to use a computer application depends upon students' prior knowledge of the material you are teaching. A study was conducted with students learning to use a database program. Students in one condition were given worked-out examples of how to use the program; students in the other condition explored use of the program in a discovery fashion. Classroom instruction in the computer application preceded students' participation in the two conditions. The results showed that worked-out examples were much more efficient with students who had limited prior knowledge, while this benefit evaporated for students with more prior knowledge. Students who had prior knowledge were able to activate and use it during discovery learning, thereby enhancing their efficiency.

Classroom Applications

Teachers may want to group students homogeneously for learning to use computer applications based on their prior knowledge, so that more experienced students use discovery learning, while less experienced students start with worked-out examples.

Teachers could also group students heterogeneously, having more experienced students work with less experienced students during discovery learning, so that the more experienced students can teach or guide the less experienced students in their discovery learning.

Precautions and Possible Pitfalls

If a teacher decides to group students homogeneously, don't keep students working permanently using worked-out examples. Once they have experience in the content area, a teacher should encourage them to apply what they have learned through discovery learning.

Source

Tuovinen, J. E., & Sweller, J. (1999). A comparison of cognitive load associated with discovery learning and worked examples. *Journal of Educational Psychology, 91*(2), 334-341.

Strategy 74: Understand that technology in the classroom is more than word processing.

What the Research Says

A nationwide survey of over 4,000 teachers found that in the 1997-1998 school year, the most commonly assigned use of technology in the classroom was still word processing— required by nearly 50% of the teachers (Becker, 1999). It appears that despite gains in incorporating the use of technology into U.S. schools, many teachers and students either are not using the technology available to them or are using technology for projects that could be done offline more quickly and with less effort extraneous to the learning content (Healy, 1998).

Classroom Applications

Many new teachers coming out of teacher education programs are now required, as part of their credentialing process, to be competent in using computers and basic network technology. Most schools today have at least one computer in the classroom and a computer lab for student use. A few schools in Michigan give all students their own laptops to use at school and at home.

With the explosion of the Internet, teachers and students have almost a limitless amount of information available to them on the World Wide Web. Software is available for using spreadsheets and calculating and tracking student grades, and some even include programs that will type a student's paper by voice command.

Teachers should connect with their school technology person to best determine how the available technology at their site can support meaningful learning. This exploration can include connections to outside experts; collaboration between students (such as e-mail penpals), scaffolds for problem solving, visualization, and analysis tools provide opportunities for feedback, reflection, and revision.

Precautions and Possible Pitfalls

With the tremendous amount of information available to students and teachers on the Internet comes some cautionary advice. The incidence of students plagiarizing papers directly from the Internet has increased. Firewalls or filters are in place in most schools, so students do not have access to inappropriate sites (unfortunately many of these same students have unlimited access to inappropriate Web sites at home). In addition, teaching students how to determine if an Internet source is valid and meaningful is sometimes overlooked. Two sites are recommended for assessing Web site information (because not everything that is on the Web is a fact, even if it is presented as such). One is a site from New Mexico State University Library (lib.nmsu.edu/instruction/eval.html). This site details exactly what Web users should look for when assessing a site. There are also suggestions for teachers to use when planning Internet-based assignments. The "T is for Thinking" site at the ICYou See Guide to Critical Thinking (www.ithaca.edu/library/Training/hott.html) has lots of links to sites that illustrate the lesson the guide is discussing. This site is geared toward students, complete with homework and a pop quiz.

There is no doubt the use of technology in the classroom will increase greatly in the future. The impact and potential for helping students prepare to meet the challenges of the real world when schools incorporate the technology of the future with the combination of traditional face-to-face instruction will be limitless.

Sources

Becker, H. J. (1999). *Internet use by teachers: Conditions of professional use and teacher-directed use*. Irvine, CA: Center for Research on Information Technology and Organizations.

Healy, J. (1998). *Failure to connect: How computers affect our children's minds—for better and worse*. New York: Simon & Schuster.

Means, B., & Olson, K. (1999). Technology's role in student-centered classrooms. In H. Walberg & H. Waman (Eds.), *New directions for teaching practice and research* (pp.297-319). Berkeley, CA: McCutchan.

 Strategy 75: Take advantage of teacher support Web sites. They can help you avoid reinventing the wheel.

What the Research Says

Teachers have more information available to them on the Internet to assist them in lesson planning, subject area content, and problem solving than ever before. As access to this technology grows, teachers must decide how best to use it. For a teacher who is new to the profession, it is advantageous to use information about best practices that is already available and has been used successfully by other teachers. *How People Learn*, a recent report from the National Research Council (Bransford, Brown, & Cocking, 1999), applies principles from research on human learning to issues of education. It is not necessary for every lesson, strategy, and activity to be original. Teachers by their very nature are sharing individuals, and there are many Web sites geared specifically to assist new teachers.

Classroom Applications

 No doubt many beginning teachers feel overwhelmed by the scope of their chosen profession. Collaborating with a mentor or colleague can help ease some of the frustrations and problems new teachers may encounter. They may also gain insight and ideas for lessons and classroom management tips from a seasoned veteran. But what about after school hours or when a teacher is home alone at 10 p.m.? Where can a new teacher turn for help and advice from other teachers? The Internet has changed the way we communicate, socialize, shop, and stay informed. There are also some Web sites geared toward helping new teachers succeed. Sites such as "Teachers Helping Teachers" (www.pacificnet.net/~mandel) is by teachers and for teachers. Its goal is to provide to beginning teachers some basic tips that can be used immediately in the classroom. The site offers lesson plans and a list of educational Web sites organized by subject area and topic. "The Beginning Teacher's Tool Box" (www.inspiringteachers.com) is a site operated by veteran teachers of the Inspiring Teachers Publishing Group in Garland, Texas. This site offers everything from "Ask Our Mentor a Question" to "Tips for New Teachers." Included in this site are words of inspiration, humor, and a list of the top 10 things to do before school starts.

Over 2,000 lesson plans organized by grade, subject, and keyword can be accessed at the PBS Teacher Source (www.pbs.org/teachersource/search.htm). All content areas are represented and teachers can see how the lessons match many national, state, and district standards.

There are two Web sites that are a "must" for the new teacher. First is Kathy Schrock's "Guide for Educators" (discoveryschool.com/schrockguide), an extremely comprehensive site that hosts a wide range of topics that are organized in a user-friendly manner. The second is a site that every teacher, beginning or veteran, should know about. The U.S. Department of Education's Web site, "The New Teacher's Guide to the U. S. Department of Education" (ed.gov/pubs/TeachersGuide), provides a wealth of information free of charge.

Precautions and Possible Pitfalls

The use of the Internet in the past few years has changed the way that teachers view the world. While there is a plethora of Internet Web sites catering to teachers, students, and education, it is important for the beginning teacher not to become caught up in a site that can simply provide busywork for students. Care should be taken to determine the validity of site information while allowing teachers a practical look at the information presented.

Sources

Bransford, J. D., Brown, A. L., & Cocking, R. R. (Eds.). (1999). *How people learn: Brain, mind, experience, and school.* Washington, DC: National Academy Press.

Eckman, A. (2001). Web wonders: Teaching the Internet generation. *Association for Supervision and Curriculum Development Bulletin, 58*(2), 96-97.

Kelly, L. (1999). Web wonders. *Association for Supervision and Curriculum Development Bulletin, 56*(8), 83-84.

9

Enhancing Teacher Self-Assessment and Reflection

Strategy 76: Look behind the scenes when assessing the teaching styles of others. Use first impressions as triggers to learn more about the rationale and philosophy behind the teaching styles you observe.

What the Research Says

Once leaving the confines of a college or university classroom, new teachers are often confronted with a range of teaching styles that they may not be familiar with. This can be a confusing time as many times the college or university programs have defined teaching styles and techniques that are deemed the "correct" way to teach and may be very different than what a new teacher is confronted with in the real world.

This article (Black & Davern, 1998) describes scenarios where new teachers were confronted with confusing classroom situations that became so distracting that the new teacher failed to see the innovative aspects of the particular classroom. The article goes further to describe a communication breakdown that begins with new teachers failing to ask host teachers questions that would have helped them to see the "method behind the madness" in what they were observing and experiencing, usually for the first time.

For example, it is very common to see problem-based pedagogy or discovery learning techniques in classrooms these days. Kids are out of their seats, working in teams, and the noise level can be high. To a novice it can look like nothing constructive is taking place, yet to a veteran teacher it is a controlled and orchestrated teaching and learning environment. Various teaching strategies can be seen in such classrooms such as cooperative grouping, sophisticated teaming skills, mutual learning, learning self-regulatory skills, self-pacing, and competitive strategies. Yes, students are out of their seats and not all the students seem to be engaged, but the majority are. Having students sitting quietly in their desks doesn't ensure everyone is on task either.

University supervisors critiqued the scenarios that were used in the research to show how novice teachers could easily misread valid learning and teaching strategies.

Classroom Applications

Careful analysis of the overall character of a class activity, lesson, or strategy can help a novice teacher focus on the details. Don't let your first impressions define what is going on. List your questions and analyze them as best you can and be ready to discuss them with the classroom teacher. Critiquing teaching practices is a skill in itself and needs to be learned. It will become a valuable skill. Ultimately it is important to make distinctions between those practices you would use and incorporate into your own repertoire and those you would not.

Without appearing judgmental, ask the teacher or teachers involved why he or she chose a specific teaching strategy. Once you become aware of possibly new perspectives, you become free to learn from them and to apply them to your own instructional practices.

Strategies for successful observations include the following:

• Listen carefully to the concerns of the teacher you are observing. Practice presenting a message to them that indicates you are interested and want to discuss issues freely, nonjudgmentally, constructively, and openly.

• Model respect and appreciation for the challenges that school staff experience. Go behind the instructional scenes and ask what the teacher educator needed to do before the observation and what resources were needed to get to this point in time with the students.

● Explore the teacher's perceptions of the needs of the class to help validate what is happening in the classroom. Explore the strengths and weaknesses of the strategies used.

● Articulate your own teaching practices and philosophies to veteran teachers. Practice skillful ways of raising difficult subjects. Realize differences are inevitable within any staff. Nurture your spirit of independent thought and learn to diplomatically raise differences you may have regarding practices and philosophies. Develop a critical analytic ability and reflective skills to help identify, explore, and articulate your ideas.

Precautions and Possible Pitfalls

 Some veteran teachers may not be as receptive to questioning as you would like. Don't take it personally. Hopefully all your contacts will be positive and useful. As with any profession, there is a range of competency among teachers, and not every contact you make may click with you. Also, teachers are not "good" or "bad" all the time. They have good and bad days, successful and not so successful lessons. Classes of students can also have bad days where nothing seems to work. Proms, dances, Fridays, Mondays, sporting events, weather, and a range of other factors can affect a specific lesson or observation on any given day.

Source

Black, A., & Davern, L. (1998). When a preservice teacher meets the classroom team (managing conflicts of teacher strategies). *Educational Leadership, 55*(5), 55.

 Strategy 77: Reflect on how your personal organizational and management lifestyle can affect your teaching performance and student achievement in your classes.

What the Research Says

Determining the potential impact of a teacher's lifestyle, especially the teacher's organizational approach to life, could be very useful to teachers and teacher educators. This study focused on assessing whether a teacher's organizational lifestyle could predict teacher performance in areas that were clearly related to student achievement.

The study was conducted at a comprehensive southeastern state university. Seventy-five students who were engaged in student teaching in a variety of public school settings, ranging from kindergarten through high school, took part in this study. Five university supervisors, with an average of 15 student teachers assigned to each, also participated in the research. Of the student participants, 52 were male and 23 were female.

Each teacher subject was given a Life Style Approach Inventory to assess organizational style and self-management. They were also given the Teacher Performance Appraisal Instrument as a measure of teacher behaviors that have been found in research literature to be positively correlated with student achievement.

The researchers concluded that student teachers who reported being the most and least organized also tended to receive the highest and lowest ratings for their teaching performance. It was also suggested that higher scores on the Life Style Approach Inventory were also positively associated with life satisfaction, self-efficacy, optimism, and positive health, and lower scores were associated with stress and poor health.

Classroom Applications

In the early phases of your teaching career, self-analyze your approach to life (both globally and specifically) and use the information as a basis for changing behaviors that are related to and directly affect your teaching. Teachers often cite a variety of factors *other than themselves* that contribute to the difficulties of schools. In a second survey of attitudes toward public schools, teachers cited lack of parental interest, lack of proper financial support, lack of student interest, and lack of discipline as being the biggest problems facing public schools. However, much of what happens and is accomplished in the classroom is a product of the teacher's performance.

Teachers bring with them an organizational lifestyle approach that affects their performance and probably the achievement of their students. Those teachers who have a clear focus on what they want to achieve and an effective time-management style in completing tasks support pathways toward achievement and bring an organized approach that is reflected in behaviors in teaching. Achieving an organized lifestyle will influence teaching performance, and those scoring highest on the Life Style Approach Inventory were also most likely to believe their behaviors influence performance.

Precautions and Possible Pitfalls

This thinking and reflection should not be used to predict a person's aptitude for teaching. Like flaws in sports techniques, it should be used to analyze flaws in teaching techniques that don't contribute to student achievement and teacher well-being. It also supports a view of the teacher assuming responsibility for the classroom outcomes rather than exporting the responsibility to other factors.

Source

Long, J. D., & Gaynor, P. (1993). Organizational life style as a predictor of student teaching performance. *Education*, *113*(3), 2-5.

Strategy 78: Don't let everyday activities obscure class goals and long-term objectives. To serve as points of reflection, have students create a portfolio format based on a course syllabus or with rubric-style class goals and objectives.

What the Research Says

Student assessment through portfolios is becoming popular. However, there is little guidance for the creation of portfolios in some disciplines. One model involved a record of individual student goals and objectives and whether they were achieved, a record of student grades, a self-evaluation form, and work samples within a high school chemistry class. This portfolio model demonstrates student progression while also engaging students in personal reflection on their class experiences and learning processes. The research found that student responses at teacher-student conferences dealing with personal goals and objectives have been positive and much of the subjectivity is avoided.

Classroom Applications

A portfolio of this type seems like a logical extension of the rubric or class syllabus philosophy. The main question here is who develops the balance between a teacher-centered or student-centered approach to goal and objective creation? Consider the creation of a class-designed portfolio facilitated and managed collaboratively. Teachers have certain content and process requirements based on school, state, and national expectations for performance. The major goals of constructing a portfolio of this type is to clearly illustrate and communicate the goals of instruction and engage students in the role of self-assessment.

Ideally, the students' goals will be combined with the teacher-mandated goals. Student goals might feature class-generated, more personal goals that form a student-centered working guideline shared by all stakeholders. This might consider and include the academic side as well as a more metacognitive side.

Once agreed upon, the portfolio (rubric or syllabus format) document becomes a class academic guide that students, teachers, and parents can relate to, visit, and revisit as needed to discover where they are on the educational map within the class.

Teachers can develop their own curricular guide for a period of time within the class to help students keep clear goals in mind for themselves as they acquire discipline knowledge and process skills. Teacher-student conferences can help teachers and students mutually assess progress. Consider doing a partial guide-rubric-syllabus and have the students add their own personal goals and objectives to help them define the type of literacy they hope to achieve. Theirs could end up looking very different than yours. It would be interesting to have students do this at the beginning of a class to help you get a feel for their expectations for teaching and learning in your class.

Precautions and Possible Pitfalls

A document such as that described has a way of becoming obsolete as class conditions change. Be prepared to revisit the portfolio framework as needed. Adjustments will need to be made. Be prepared to share the responsibility for this as needed. Goals and objectives that seem feasible early may need to be mediated. Experience over time will help the process evolve, and your comfort level with this assessment tool will increase.

Sources

Adamchik, C. (1996). The design and assessment of chemistry portfolios. *Journal of Chemical Education, 73*(6), 528-530.

Hebert, E. (1998). Lessons learned about student portfolios. *Phi Delta Kappan, 79*(8), 583-585.

Strategy 79: Explore and discover the natural teaching styles within yourself. Teaching style is something you find within yourself and not something supervising teachers or college or university education programs give you.

What the Research Says

"Hope you have a reasonable class so you would be more of yourself. Keep it real!"

This powerful quote came from a student teacher's journal (Rotanz, 2001). A student in her class gave this quote to Rotanz. This special student helped her, with her popularity and leadership, and loud voice, control her first assigned class. The student teacher went on to say that she had not recognized her student's accurate perception of her own struggles to suppress her identity according to the instructions given to her by her partnership teacher. She went on to describe how her partnership teacher made it clear that her natural personality was not consistent with that of a "real teacher." The partnership teacher felt that she was "too approachable" in laughing with the students or speaking less formally. As a student teacher she also shelved her concerns for the partnership teacher's lenient grading policies and decontextualized assignments. She felt she was only able to make decisions if they agreed with her partnership teacher. Her practice teaching had her using methods she found she didn't believe in.

While the referenced paper was not classic research in a formal sense, it does illustrate the dilemma that many new teachers find themselves in. Rotanz used her reflective journal entries to conclude that student teaching can be a very divisive activity as those that are there for support can actually stymie new teachers' development in finding out who they are as teachers. She went on to point out situations that contributed to her negative feeling and emotional reactions to her relationship with her partnership teacher.

Experiences such as she described in her article act to demoralize a new teacher who looks to his or her partnership teacher or university preparation as golden. She also went on to reflect about the lack of respect most teachers at her site had for her university training. She came to realize that the reality of the site and a real classroom was something she wasn't really prepared for. She also realized that the very people that were there for support hindered her development as a teacher and student collaborator.

Classroom Applications

The article points out a situation and dilemma that many student teachers and some new teachers find themselves in. The true point of student teaching is to work with guides that help you to find yourself and protect you from gross mistakes. You're not there to clone yourself after their style or the work of others. It is more of an exploration and blending of tactics that fits your own professional style. Teachers new to the profession often don't know they have had a bad experience as a student teacher until it is over. The key here is to work for a placement based on some mutual compatibility. To do this you need information. That means you have to voice your concerns to the correct person, whether it is a principal or a university or college supervisor. Sometimes college or university education teachers know the schools in their area and can suggest schools based on what they know about you and the school. If you're lucky they can suggest a principal and maybe even a teacher within your content area.

Take time to reflect on teaching and learning methods, styles, and techniques that make sense to you and try to find placements that help you hone your best guess at how you want to plan instruction and teach.

Precautions and Possible Pitfalls

My first placement put me in an art room with a master teacher who expected me to use lessons that she created and had been using for years. I didn't create anything new in projects or assessments. I couldn't do what she did some of the time or do it as well as she did most of the time. I felt horrible because everything I did was subpar. She wanted all her classes to experience the same projects and instructional strategies. Therefore I was stuck and missed out on half of the experiences new teachers are supposed to have, such as creating your own learning and teaching pathways. What do you do for a backup plan when the ideal placement doesn't come along or turns sour? Quick communication works best here.

I could have avoided this placement if I didn't blindly accept it. Mitigate and compromise with those responsible for your supervision. Find out what their expectations are and whether you share them. Often their letters of recommendation carry weight and you want a good one, so your performance is important. A good supporting teacher is a guide on the side and mentor, not a blueprint to copy. After teaching for awhile I came to the conclusion that it takes three trips through a lesson or project to really get it down. It also differs with the student mix you get. My master teacher's expectations were beyond my reach and my placement was a recipe for failure.

However, my university supervisor recognized the mistake and supported me through the experience. He said he would make sure no other new teachers would be placed with my master teacher. However, it did some damage to my ego and development as a teacher. I still see my second master teacher 25 years later. She let me plan and deliver my own lessons and find myself. She laughed at my mistakes, offered suggestions on how I could improve my lessons and strategies, and became a good friend.

Source

Rotanz, L. (2001). Breaking free of the puppeteer: Perspectives on one practice teacher's experience. *High School Journal. 84*(3), 19-25.

 Strategy 80: Reflect upon teaching components that reach beyond lesson delivery and assessment. Constant reflection about teaching practice is what effective veteran teachers do.

What the Research Says

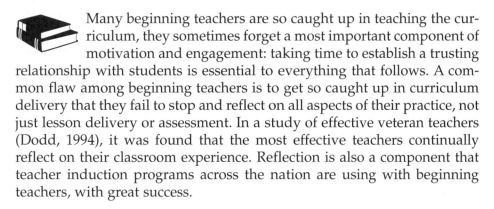 Many beginning teachers are so caught up in teaching the curriculum, they sometimes forget a most important component of motivation and engagement: taking time to establish a trusting relationship with students is essential to everything that follows. A common flaw among beginning teachers is to get so caught up in curriculum delivery that they fail to stop and reflect on all aspects of their practice, not just lesson delivery or assessment. In a study of effective veteran teachers (Dodd, 1994), it was found that the most effective teachers continually reflect on their classroom experience. Reflection is also a component that teacher induction programs across the nation are using with beginning teachers, with great success.

Classroom Applications

 Some questions effective teachers might ask themselves through reflection are as follows. Is rapport and trust, essential to a successful classroom environment, developing with their students? Did the lesson presented accomplish its objective? Was students' prior knowledge connected with the learning goals? How did the teacher promote social development and group responsibility? By reflecting on not just the lesson but on all aspects of their teaching, teachers can create classes where students are engaged, feel supported, and are successful. Taking a few minutes after each lesson to reflect, and then record the aspects of the day that were successful or needed improvement, can be a valuable exercise. The teacher should note lesson pacing and organization, student involvement, ongoing assessment techniques, environmental issues, and comfort with material. Teachers should also not downplay the importance of taking time to develop and nurture trust between the teacher and the students. One way to begin to develop this trust is by simply giving students a sort of questionnaire. On this questionnaire are the typical questions such as name, address, home phone, and class schedule (if a middle or secondary school). Other important information that may assist the teacher is parent(s) or guardian(s) name (this is especially important if the parent or guardian's last name is different than the student's). Questions such as, "What do I as your teacher need to know about you to help you succeed in this class?" may provide the teacher insight into factors that could prevent the student from learning, such as parents going through a divorce, a parent just lost a job, the student is in foster care, or a parent is seriously ill. The student might also be terrified of reading out loud or speaking in front of the class. Teachers will be surprised at the candor students will relate if only they're given the opportunity. Along these same lines, questions asking about hobbies, sports, or a job after school may help explain when a student seems overly stressed or when homework isn't complete. Having this information and reflecting upon the potential impact on class instruction can help the novice teacher grow both personally and professionally. The reflection does not have to be lengthy or formal but should be consistent. The insights gained should then be used to adapt and refine the novice teacher's practice.

Precautions and Possible Pitfalls

Many novice (and veteran) teachers are reluctant to reflect on a lesson or assessment because of the potential for criticism. This is especially true if the reflection is being shared with another teacher. Not wanting to appear anything but perfect in front of other teachers may prevent new teachers from venturing outside the traditional venues of instruction. However, many times, the lesson or test we learn the most from is not the one that is successful, but the one that fails. Beginning teachers must not be afraid to take risks. As they learn more about how their students think and feel, they will be able to adapt and create lessons where students are engaged and meaningful learning is taking place.

Source

Dodd, A. W. (1994). Learning to read the classroom: The stages leading to teacher self-actualization. *Northwards*, 4,13-26.

10

Developing
a Professional
Identity

 Strategy 81: Learn how to accept not knowing in the classroom setting. A new teacher needs to develop a tolerance and comfort level for this.

What the Research Says

In a study of four female teachers (Schmidt & Knowles, 1995) who experienced failure as beginning teachers, "not knowing" was seen as a major contributor to the panic they felt. Because these new teachers had been very successful students in their teacher education courses, they believed they should have learned enough to succeed in their initial teaching situations. All four learned to manage the world of academic knowledge where right answers were expected and identifiable. However, these women did not recognize, nor did their mentors articulate, that the classroom trenches were more complex and unpredictable than college and university education classes.

The researchers were all unaware of the deep panic caused by the women's sense of not knowing and the paralysis and uneasiness they felt at not being able to define options or understand the advice their mentors gave them. Often the advice did not match their own perceptions of teaching and thus contributed to vague understandings of themselves as teachers.

All four had experienced the classroom themselves as obedient, compliant students and held dysfunctional understandings of the teacher's role—in particular, the nature of authority in the classroom. Their own experiences taught them to equate a teacher's disapproval with a broken relationship and, as women, to avoid provoking such a situation. Their roles as compliant students, attempting to please everyone around them, contributed to their problems in classroom relationships and management. They had trouble finding models of authority that did not feel like they were being mean or bad.

They had trouble learning to live more comfortably with insoluble dilemmas of everyday teaching and the large number of variable factors that contribute to the complexity of everyday problems. They might have better understood that that not knowing is a function of learning rather than a function of incompetence. It is a legitimate and sometimes exciting state for teachers, and asking good questions is more important than having the right answers. The research findings suggest that compliant students, particularly those that appear shy and unassertive, may need more and different experiences to gain confidence, independence, and competence as student teachers. While the study focused on four women, gender was merely symptomatic of more basic beliefs from their experiences as students in schools and as children in families.

Classroom Applications

All teachers come with baggage from their own experiences as students. Most teachers like school and were successful in the classroom as students. Beginning teachers often have a difficult time understanding students who do not share their view of the school and classroom. They are presented with students they may have not associated with themselves. These same groups of students they may have been intimidated by or didn't like as students themselves are now there for them to manage as authoritarian teachers. Not knowing how to deal with these situations can add to a teacher's feeling of failure, and most teacher education programs haven't prepared teachers to face these situations.

This is especially true for many women, especially those who were shy, unassertive, and overly compliant as students. Confronting the students' management and discipline issues is often difficult for women from this background. Because these women attempted to please nearly everyone around them, who they wanted to be was generally overshadowed by their desire to be what others expected them to be.

- The first suggestion or strategy is to develop a sense of reflection with these factors in mind. New teachers need to explore their own personal history as students. It is easier to begin to identify factors that inhibit management strategies in advance than in retrospect. Teachers will have to manage students whom they may not understand or would have not socialized with as students. At times a new teacher's instructional techniques and management routines will be underdeveloped. The teacher will need to find models of authority that do not feel like being mean or mad or models that fit who the teacher is as a person. Teachers should begin to role-play how assertive and challenging students may confront them in the classroom.

- The second suggestion is to quickly identify and be able to articulate situations in the classroom that the teachers' background has not prepared them for. Many new teachers cope by ignoring unfamiliar problems or hoping they will not be repeated. This situation is compounded by not sharing the problem with those that could offer help, usually for fear of feeling like a failure. It is important to remember that not knowing is the first step in problem solving. As the research points out, asking good questions is more important than having the right answers.

- A mentor may offer good advice that may not fit the teacher's own self-perception as a teacher. Teachers shouldn't be afraid to modify and adjust the information mentors give to fit their own situation and personality. Remember that not all classroom problems can be solved. Even experienced teachers do not possess answers to every dilemma or student problem. Knowing when you are facing a one-time problem or a chronic expanding issue comes with experience.

- Not all the cooperating support staff whom new teachers are asked to work with are created equally. If teachers finds themselves in a placement that leaves them confused or they don't think the mentors are sensitive enough to their problems, seeking help from those who can help can be beneficial. Find others at the site who are open to a new teacher's inquiries and who would be sensitive to a new teacher's perspectives. More connected and collaborative styles of supervision help beginning teachers view their unique personal qualities and skills as contributing to success, not to perceived failure.

While the characteristics of the research featured qualities most associated with female teachers, they are not gender specific. Men can be good students, shy, and compliant, too. Becoming aware of the personal concepts of student-teacher interactions can begin to help you understand the teacher you are and the teacher you want to be. It can also begin to help explain how you perceive management relationships in your classes.

Precautions and Possible Pitfalls

The concept of failure is a powerful enemy. Like learning the skills of almost any sport, success is a product of repeated trials and errors. Teachers must be patient with themselves. Teaching is a journey not a destination. Every veteran teacher went through similar experiences. The perception of failure can usually be redefined as another necessary step toward becoming an effective teacher. This is not to say that all beginning teachers will be successful. Turn "not knowing" into a challenge and a question that can be answered with the right help, reflection, patience, and perseverance.

Source

Schmidt, M., & Knowles, G. J. (1995). Four women's stories of "failure" as beginning teachers. *Teaching and Teacher Education, 11*(5), 429-444.

Strategy 82: Create the right perception through a teaching uniform. A teacher who dresses in a professional manner will be treated as a professional.

What the Research Says

The way teachers dress sets the stage for what will later occur in their classrooms. Wong and Wong (1991) urge teachers to make no mistake about the commonsense principle that they will be treated as they are dressed. Research also shows that dress is of great importance in the business world, where there is no vacillation about insisting on an expected standard of dress. This is not to say that teachers should wear a uniform; however, whether they like it or not teachers are models in every facet of their job, including the way they dress. As children become older, they become increasingly able to remember, and then practice, that which they see modeled.

Classroom Applications

A teacher seeking a job would never go to an interview in anything other than the most professional attire. In fact, most administrators say a candidate's attire influences their decision in the interview process. However, once teachers are hired, particularly if they are young or close in age to the students, they may resort to casual attire. This choice of dress can sometimes even look very similar to the clothing the students are wearing. Some beginning teachers have the notion they should dress so the students will like them and show their "with-it-ness." Students don't need to like their teachers, but they do need to respect them. Teachers are role models and should be concerned about their dress for several reasons. First, the way a teacher is dressed makes a statement about who that person is. Secretly, teachers' dress also sends a message about their expectations. Second, if we are to be considered professionals, we must dress like professionals. Certainly a person's manner of dress has great significance in the business world where there seems to be no doubt about an expected standard of dress. This is not to say teachers should have uniformity in the way they dress. However, certain commonsense standards seem clear. It is not necessary to dress in one's "Sunday best," but a shirt and tie for men and slacks or a skirt with a blouse or sweater for women can help create a positive image. Women should leave the very short skirts, low cut blouses, shorts, and tight stretch pants at home. A thoughtful, reasonable, and well-planned wardrobe is all that is necessary. The message to students will help establish credibility and contribute to an effective learning environment.

As a new teacher, the challenges are great. By making dress work for you rather than against you, the signals are clear—those who want respect for themselves and their profession must dress accordingly.

Precautions and Possible Pitfalls

Given the fact that most schools do not have a dress code for teachers, and because of the legal implications of the possible infringement on personal liberties, it is difficult to enforce professional dress for teachers. Frequently teachers will cite low pay as one of the reasons they don't dress more professionally. However, one has only to look at school secretaries and support staff (who usually make much less than teachers) to see a standard of professional dress. Conversely, if the principal dresses as casually, sloppily, or provocatively as some teachers do, their credibility and respect from teachers and the community might be suspect. Beginning teachers, especially if they are young, can benefit from every possible advantage. Dressing in a professional business-like manner won't make someone a better teacher, but it does set the stage for what will subsequently happen in the classroom.

Sources

Siefert, K., and Hoffnung, R. (1991). Child and adolescent development. Boston: Houghton Mifflin.

Wong, H., and Wong, R. (1991). *The first days of school.* Sunnyvale, CA: Harry K. Wong.

 Strategy 83: Take time to recognize and remedy stressful situations.

What the Research Says

 Many studies have been performed over the years that have documented high levels of stress and burnout in schoolteachers. Sources of teacher stress may include time demands, large class sizes, mountains of paperwork, difficulties with misbehaving students, financial constraints, and lack of educational supplies.

Teacher stress and burnout is a consideration for many educators (and it certainly should be for the general population as we face huge teacher shortages in the areas of mathematics, science, and special education nationwide). The stress some teachers face can lead to physical and emotional exhaustion. The consequences can include less job satisfaction, lessened student-teacher rapport, and decreased teacher effectiveness in meeting the needs of students.

Classroom Applications

There is no doubt that the first years of teaching are often extremely challenging and stressful. With increased demands for more accountability as measured by standardized testing, less parental involvement, and more time demands being placed on teachers, the need for teachers to take care of themselves has never been greater.

Teachers must make time for themselves to deal with the everyday stresses of teaching. The idea must be one of working smarter, not harder. Frequently, new teachers complain that if only there were more hours in the day to get things accomplished they wouldn't be so stressed; however, the answer is not to find more hours in a day, but instead to organize those hours they already have in a way that is both healthy and productive. One way to help decrease stress is to connect with a mentor or colleague in the same department or building who can help with organizing and planning of curriculum. The new teacher cannot be afraid to share concerns or ask for help. They can receive advice and suggestions from exemplary veterans so there is not a continual reinventing of the wheel. The beginning teacher can get help in prioritizing and organizing what needs to be done. It is not necessary to grade every single paper that comes across the teacher's desk. Sometimes a checkmark on the assignment or activity to note it was completed is sufficient. Computer software grading systems, which also allow the teacher to enter grades, print out individual student reports, and post class grades, can be a tremendous timesaver.

The teacher who wants to work until caught up should buy a sofabed, set it up in the classroom, and have the phone number of Pizza Hut on speed dial, as the in-basket will never be empty. Veteran teachers know not to plan large assignments near the end of grading periods so as not to pull all-nighters grading student work. The new teacher should also definitely think about a "no late work" policy before school starts to avoid having an additional pile of paperwork to grade right before report cards are due.

Economic concerns may be remedied by asking for help. Many schools are receiving help from parent and community groups which supplement educational resources with wish lists or mini-grants ranging from the basics such as construction paper, white board markers, and Kleenex to class sets of dictionaries, supplemental texts, and VCRs. As a new teacher it is critical to explore these additional resources.

Another key factor to help reduce stress is to develop and teach (just like any other lesson) the rules and procedures for maintaining classroom control. Too often new teachers are heard to say that they don't have time to teach rules and procedures because the class must be to chapter 37 by March. The reality is that if classroom rules and procedures are not in place and effective, there will be little actual learning taking place. The result will be increased frustration for both the teacher and the students. Not taking the time to teach rules and procedures could also force a teacher to buy Maalox in the large economy size to keep in a desk drawer.

Diet, rest, and exercise can be extremely helpful in reducing stress. Eating a well-balanced diet, getting a good night's sleep, and exercising are all known to be essential for good health. However, sometimes as a new teacher, taking care of oneself is the first area to be compromised. A daily multivitamin can help when a well-balanced diet is not always possible. Just as teachers make time to grade and prepare lesson plans, so too should they make time for exercise. Reducing stress can be as simple as taking a brisk walk around the block, attending a yoga class, or working out at the gym. The effects of exercise can give teachers time for reflection, clear the mind, and help the teacher to reorganize priorities.

Precautions and Possible Pitfalls

⚠ Stress and burnout in teaching are usually not the result of one event, but rather are the continual process in which environmental forces threaten a teacher's well-being. Stress can also be exacerbated by unrealistic demands the teachers place on themselves. It is unrealistic for any new teacher to expect to perform at the level of an experienced teacher. It is, therefore, crucial to teacher success to be able to share concerns with others. The use of mentors can help by giving new teachers an outlet for expression while capitalizing on opportunities to learn what they are doing right and give them support when problems arise. Mentors can also share their own struggles and frustrations as new teachers and offer solutions by sharing the ways they overcame their problems.

The first years of teaching are a time for the beginning teacher to develop both as a person and as a professional. With almost half of new teachers leaving the profession in the first three years, it is imperative to give every manner of support possible in helping reduce stress and burnout.

Sources

Coates, T. J., & Thorsen, C. E. (1976). Teacher anxiety: A review with recommendations. *Review of Educational Research, 46*, 159-184.

Kyriacou, C. (1987). Teacher stress and burnout: An international review. *Educational Research, 29*, 146-152.

Kyriacou, C., & Sutcliffe, J. (1987). Teacher stress: Prevalence, sources, and symptoms. *British Journal of Educational Psychology, 48*, 159-167.

11

Enhancing
Professional
Relationships
With Colleagues

 Strategy 84: *Avoid burnout by choosing your mentors carefully.*

What the Research Says

Teacher burnout is a well-documented and well-known phenomenon. In the media, in magazines, on television, and in research, burnout receives considerable attention. Research in Europe estimates that 60-70% of teachers are classified as "under frequent stress" and that approximately 30% of teachers show signs of burnout (Rudow, 1999). In the Netherlands, mental health problems appear in 36% of the cases that ultimately end up receiving a disability pension in work-incapacitated teachers (USZO, 1998). In addition, in comparisons with others that do "people work," such as mental health workers and other health professionals, teachers appear to be at high risk for burnout. Teachers report more burnout symptoms than other workers in social professions.

In this study it was hypothesized that a teacher's perceived superiority would be reduced among individuals high in burnout, especially with respect to positive behaviors. To carry the idea further, it was hypothesized that individuals high in burnout would be able to maintain a negative sense of superiority (feeling less bad than others). One hundred twenty secondary school teachers were asked to generate information about feeling inferior and superior in relationship to others. To no surprise to the researchers, only positive superiority was reduced among teachers high in burnout. They felt less good, but also less bad than others.

In summary, this research indicates that teacher burnout is accompanied by a lack of perceived superiority with respect to positive behaviors that may have a range of consequences for both teachers and their classroom environments. Teachers in a state of burnout do feel superior on negative behaviors, and this contributes to the maintenance or repair of feeling a lack of superiority. Thus, burnouts may use their colleagues' flaws and failures to boost their own self-esteem and to possibly prevent a decline in their performance as a teacher. Maslach and Jackson (1981) define burnout in a multidimensional fashion characterized by three qualities:

1. Emotional exhaustion: A depletion of emotional resources, feeling empty or worn-out.

2. Depersonalization: Characterized by negative and cynical attitudes to students.

3. A reduced sense of personal accomplishment: Individuals in burnout assess their accomplishments in negative terms.

The research concluded that burnout contributed to lower student achievement as students were perceptive and very aware of the burned-out teacher's state of mind. Other interesting comments included reflection that school culture fosters burnout when administration enforces clearly defined, narrow, measurable goals on teachers for academic achievement. Schools without these strict goals seem to give teachers more opportunity for experimenting with new teaching and learning methods that foster a more collaborative and supportive relationship with administration, thus seeing fewer symptoms of burnout.

Classroom Applications

New teachers should be aware of the phenomenon of burnout and its related symptoms. The first recommendation is that new teachers (or any teacher new to a district or school) quickly size up the professional environment they encounter and avoid forming professional relationships with teachers that offer limited support and resources due to potential burnout.

Nothing is less rewarding than to find a beginning teacher on a committee or in a working situation in a school where it is "not cool" to be professionally enthusiastic about the job. The concept of teachers as professionals has always been debated (usually outside the teaching profession). In these days of prescribed curriculum and standardized tests, curriculum choices become less and less the role of the teacher. Where teachers do have control is in the area of how curriculum is taught. In the heterogeneous mix of today's classroom, determining how is much more important than ever. Because of this, good teachers are required to be more professionally savvy than ever.

As a new teacher, don't compromise your professional enthusiasm to better fit in. Seek out other like-thinkers to avoid the symptoms of burnout presented in the research. There is a term called *communal orientation* that refers to individuals who care for and are concerned for other people. Nurses who care for their patients or have concern for them tend to experience less burnout. Overlay the same idea onto the student-teacher relationship. The one characteristic of burnout that teachers exhibit little control over is in an inequitable relationship where teachers invest more care than the recipients of the care, the students. Teachers need to find ways to understand and cope with this.

Here are some ideas that can contribute to a new teacher's sense of professional responsibility:

- Spend more time talking with colleagues about ideas, not students.
- Decentralize and focus more on students' needs than on how the teacher is perceived by students and others (this takes time!).
- The new teacher can become involved and offer services on school or district curriculum writing projects or other projects.
- Teachers should have a working knowledge of county or statewide educational issues or programs they might want to become involved with both in their content area and in education in general.
- Become involved with students in nonclassroom activities (sports, clubs, etc.)

Precautions and Possible Pitfalls

All teachers occasionally feel some of the symptoms of burnout. A professional perspective is something that is created and developed, and it continually needs maintenance. One of the warnings the researchers gave was that teachers feeling symptoms of burnout should not try to remedy the situation by working harder. They felt that by working harder teachers just added to their feeling of frustration. The idea is to not work harder but to work smarter and more efficiently. Find strategies to reduce the mundane and focus on the more creative and satisfying aspects of the teaching profession.

Sources

Brenninkmeijer, V., Vanyperen, N. W., & Buunk, B. P. (2001). I am not a better teacher, but others are doing worse: Burnout and perceptions of superiority among teachers. *Social Psychology of Education*, *4*, 259-274.

Maslach, C., & Jackson, S. (1981). The measurement of experienced burnout. *Journal of Occupational Behavior*, *2*, 99-113.

Rudow, B. (1999). Stress and burnout in the teaching profession: European studies, issues, and research perspectives. In R. Vandenberghe & A. M. Huberman (Eds.), Understanding and preventing teacher burnout: A sourcebook of international research and practice (pp. 38-58). New York: Cambridge University Press.

Uitvoeringsinstelling Sociale Zekerheid voor Overheid en Onderwijs (USZO) [Benefits Agency for the Public Service and Education Sector]. (1998). *Statistiek arbeidsongeschiktheid, Onderwijs* [Statistics incapacity for work, education]. The Netherlands: Author.

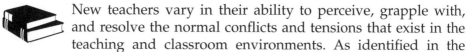

Strategy 85: Use conflict and tension as an opportunity for personal growth and change.

What the Research Says

 New teachers vary in their ability to perceive, grapple with, and resolve the normal conflicts and tensions that exist in the teaching and classroom environments. As identified in the research (Beach & Pearson, 1998), some new teachers avoid or minimize conflicts and tensions by conforming to the system or authority figure in the workplace. Others are so overwhelmed that they find conflicts and tensions unmanageable, leading to a sense of loss of control, resignation, and futility or wanting escape from the system. A review of 16 studies (Beach & Pearson, 1998) on the effectiveness of programs fostering beginning teachers' reflections found that preservice and student teachers' reflections were primarily technical or practical, with little evidence of substantial reflection (Hatton & Smith, 1995). During early student teaching experiences, focus is usually concentrated on conflicts and tensions in developing basic teaching techniques. Later in student teaching and into their first year of teaching, they shift out of their more egocentric modes of teaching, learning, and relationships to focus more on their students and their reaction to their teaching. In this study (Beach & Pearson, 1998), 28 students enrolled in a 15-month post-baccalaureate teaching program were required to reflect on their clinical experiences in journals and small-group interactions. Four basic types of conflicts and tensions were categorized:

- **Curriculum and instruction**—conflicts and tensions between planned instruction and actual events or between their perceptions and student perceptions of relevancy, or beliefs about their own teaching and curricular choices and school- or department-mandated curriculum and pedagogy.

- **Interpersonal relationships**—conflicts and tensions with and among students, other teaching colleagues, and administrators. This category could also relate to a sense of personal isolation.

- **Self-concept or role**—personal conflicts and tensions regarding the need to be accepted and well liked, the role ambiguity of transition from student to teacher, and the further definition of self.

- **Contextual and institutional**—conflicts and tensions related to the expectations of the institutions in which they work, teach, and learn. This generally involves acclimation and socialization to the culture of school and teaching.

The same research also identified three levels of strategies for coping with conflicts and tensions:

- **Avoid/denial**: In the beginning new teachers frequently described their dealings with conflicts and tensions in highly positive terms. Some assumed problems would diminish with time so they avoided coping.

- **Immediate solutions**: New teachers frequently generated short-term, quick-fix solutions. They defer tensions and conflicts between the cooperating teachers or students to the back burner. They only deal with issues when they are forced to.

- **Incorporation**: New teachers accept their conflicts and tensions as a necessary part of growth and incorporate positive changes and alteration of class and management structures to better avoid conflicts or create clear, workable mitigation plans for students. Informal professional support structures are created and integrated into interpersonal relationships with colleagues and administrators.

Precautions and Possible Pitfalls

 Good teaching is a continuous and exciting journey. If teachers think they will finally have it all down pat one day, they are mistaken. Unfortunately it is still true that new teachers often are placed in a position of trial by fire. They are given assignments that more experienced teachers would never be given. It is common to have to teach in more than one room or teach a variety of classes, forcing the new teacher to prepare for multiple settings, disciplines, and ability levels. It is hard to give advice for situations like this. In induction programs such as the Beginning Teacher Support and Assessment (BTSA) program in California, there is support for new teachers to limit the number of preparations, classroom changes, and involvement on multiple committees and coaching assignments through the first two years. It is ironic that the most inexperienced teachers are often given the most challenging assignments. Good planning and communication with all stakeholders helps.

Sources

Beach, R., & Pearson, D. (1998). Changes in preservice teachers' perceptions of conflict and tension. *Teaching and Teacher Education*, 14(3), 337-351.
Hatton, N., & Smith, D. (1995). Reflection in teacher education: Towards definition and implementation. *Teaching and Teacher Education*, 11(10), 33-49.

 Strategy 86: Exchange ideas with your colleagues as a means of professional development.

What the Research Says

Professional development has often consisted of short workshops and inservices for teachers based on needs perceived by administrators and district office personnel. Professional development is something that is often done *for* or *to* teachers instead of *with* or *by* them. All too frequently this professional development may not enhance a teacher's classroom practice.

In a study exploring a group of teachers attending monthly meetings (McCotter, 2001), researchers found that it was possible to provide new and meaningful ways of support and collegiality enabling continuous professional growth and development.

Members met monthly to provide support and feedback to one another. Support was expressed in several ways: having the opportunity to ask questions and pursue feedback, the sharing of similar experiences, suggesting solutions or strategies, or just voicing support either verbally or nonverbally. The most important characteristics of these monthly meetings consisted of a "what is said in here, stays in here" pledge, group and individual reflection and critique, seeking feedback, and all-important collaboration. Group members felt this type of professional development helped them to reflect on their practice and experiences, and more important had relevance and purpose for their classroom practice.

Classroom Application

Clearly a focus in education today is providing meaningful professional development for all stakeholders. Because beginning teachers have needs and concerns that experienced veteran teachers may not have, it is important for them to feel supported and have their problems taken seriously. Many teacher induction programs are now providing professional development specifically designed for their beginning teachers. These programs are based on needs assessments given to new teachers and on surveying teachers with a few years' experience under their belt to determine what kind of professional development would have been helpful in the first year or so of teaching. Based on this feedback, districts are tailoring programs to meet specific needs.

Many new teachers feel totally intimidated around their experienced colleagues and might be cautious, if not downright reluctant, to discuss problems or concerns for fear of being perceived as weak or not in control. When new teachers can get together in a group and share problems and concerns with their peers, they realize they are not the only one experiencing these questions or problems. The support can be as simple as giving practical suggestions for solving situations in the classroom to encouraging new teachers to step outside their comfort zone and try a new teaching strategy. The collegial communities that emerge from this ongoing support and collaboration can be lifesavers to a struggling teacher.

The use of reflective conversations with fellow beginning teachers, as well as a mentor trained in the art of reflective conversation, can also be of great benefit. This reflection should be more than just thinking back on a problem or lesson; it should operate with the purpose of changing one's practice and enhancing students' learning.

By engaging in these conversations in a nonthreatening environment, the beginning teachers have the opportunity to perceive themselves through students' eyes.

The importance of collaboration with colleagues cannot be overlooked. It is one of the most important components of good professional development for beginning teachers. If teachers new to the profession can share meaningful discussions involving a sharing of knowledge and focus on teachers' communities of practice, then as they progress from novice to experienced, confident veteran, the collaboration may well continue throughout their professional careers. The benefits, both personally and professionally, to new teachers cannot be ignored.

Precautions and Possible Pitfalls

 New teachers should be aware that professional development is not a one-size-fits-all proposition. So much advice (some good, some bad) may be thrown at them during their first few years that they need to take care not to become jaded or overwhelmed. They would also do well to distance themselves from the veteran complainers who may see all professional development opportunities as a waste of time. These are the teachers who have taught the same way for the last 25 years, haven't had a new idea or instructional strategy in that time, and can't understand why kids today aren't "getting it." Coming out of teacher education programs, teachers thinking they are equipped with all the tools and knowledge they will ever need in the classroom will be sadly disappointed. Effective and successful teachers will discover they not only participate in but also seek out professional development opportunities to continually evaluate and strive to improve their practice.

Sources

McCotter, S. S. (2001). *Collaborative groups as professional development. Teaching and Teacher Education, 17*(6), 685-704.

McLaughlin, H. J. (1996). The nature and nurture of reflection. In K. Watson, C. Modgil, & S. Modgil (Eds.), *Teachers, teacher education and training* (p. 185). New York: Cassell.

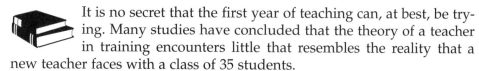

Strategy 87: Surround yourself with mentors.

What the Research Says

 It is no secret that the first year of teaching can, at best, be trying. Many studies have concluded that the theory of a teacher in training encounters little that resembles the reality that a new teacher faces with a class of 35 students.

Two conditions that can contribute to first-year difficulties are the physical and social isolation that many new teachers experience (Lortie, 1975).

Classroom Applications

Most states have some type of mentoring programs available to new teachers. It is critical for new teachers to surround themselves with exemplary experienced colleagues. In most schools, almost without exception, teachers work in settings where the sociocultural context, if not the actual physical structure, encourages little interaction among adults and can contribute to feelings of isolation and frustration. By developing a relationship with a mentor and establishing regularly scheduled times to meet and talk, the new teacher will learn to cope with the myriad of problems that may be encountered, as well as have the opportunity to learn and grow professionally. Data from California's BTSA (Beginning Teacher Support and Assessment) program indicate that ongoing collaboration and reflections between the new teachers and their mentors help new teachers gain insights, perspectives, and deeper understandings of the context and complexity of teaching while giving them the support and encouragement they so desperately need.

Precautions and Possible Pitfalls

It is critical to the success of the new teacher-mentor relationship to have mentors who are carefully selected, well trained, and accessible. Mentors need to be trained in the art of reflective conversation and really *listening* to the new teacher's concerns. What the new teacher doesn't need is a mentor who will just offer to fix the problem. Sometimes experienced teachers are more eager to offer solutions, often based on their own personal experience, rather than asking questions which help guide the problem-solving process. This technique does little to help new teachers build confidence in their own problem-solving strategies. Having a mentor who really listens and is accessible is immensely important.

Beginning teachers need to be careful of aligning with veteran teachers who are negative. This is usually someone who has been in the profession a long time, is counting the days to retirement, and has been teaching the same way for 20 years. This person is usually the one who hasn't attended a professional growth opportunity in years, feels students are an imposition, and will be eager to find a willing ear to bend. Don't let that ear be yours.

Source

Lortie, D. C. (1975). *Schoolteacher: A sociological study*. Chicago: University of Chicago.

12

Fostering
a Positive
Relationship
With Parents

 Strategy 88: Help parents understand media coverage of educational issues. Informed parents should not let media reports change their views of their own children's abilities.

What the Research Says

Parents may develop misconceptions about their children's abilities as a result of reports in the media. One study examined the impact on parents of a media report on gifted junior high school students. Extensive media coverage focused on a report of a major gender difference in students' mathematical aptitudes. The study compared parents' views about their children's mathematical aptitudes before and after exposure to the media report. The results showed that the media coverage changed parents' attitudes about their children's mathematical abilities. Fathers of sons and mothers of daughters developed stronger gender-based stereotyped beliefs after the media coverage. This can perpetuate unrealistic or limiting expectations for students.

Classroom Applications

Many students find one discipline or another to be particularly frustrating. Many parents react by saying that they didn't do well in that subject themselves, so they tend to accept this from their children. Sometimes it appears to be a sort of badge of honor to admit weakness in science or mathematics (unlike almost any other subject!). Teachers can offer periodic workshops for parents, keeping them informed of what is being taught, how it is being presented, and what can be expected of their children, both in performance and in results. This sort of workshop experience will also give teachers an opportunity to communicate with parents regularly and to inform them of their individual child's progress and ability to be successful in whatever discipline is being taught. Parents will then be more prepared to interpret reports from the media and other sources. These same parents would also be less likely to succumb to overgeneralizations and stereotypes that could undermine their child's performance.

Precautions and Possible Pitfalls

Extreme patience must be used when working with parents. Recognize that many of them may have been away from a school setting and the concomitant behavior for many years. A teacher should be cautious when reporting frequently on a student's progress. Leave room for improvement and never close the door on an individual student, no matter how frustrating the child's progress may be. It is especially important to remember that some parents have a tendency to overreact to the teacher's comments, and that may have deleterious effects.

Source

Jacobs, J. E., & Eccles, J. S. (1985). Gender differences in ability: The impact of media reports on parents. *Educational Researcher*, 14(3), 20-25.

 Strategy 89: Learn what your teacher education program didn't tell you about parent conferences. Get help from knowledgeable colleagues, master teachers, or college and university supervisors.

What the Research Says

 A questionnaire was developed to determine preservice program requirements relative to information and skills for parent-teacher conferences. One hundred thirty-six teacher education institutions were questioned. One hundred twenty-four institutions responded.

The percentages of those that frequently required preparation for parent-teacher conferencing are listed as follows:

- Elementary 59%
- Early childhood education 57%
- Special education 44%
- K-12/All levels 42%

Nineteen percent of the responding institutions provided and required a separate course for parent-teacher conferences. Seventy-five percent indicated that these skills are taught in a methods course context. Seventy percent included parent-teacher conferencing content and skills in field-based experiences.

Despite renewed emphasis on parental involvement, preservice programs did not consistently identify parent-teacher conferencing skills as a major objective. Field-based experiences address the topic but appear hindered by school policies in actual conferences.

Classroom Applications

If, as a new teacher, you do not feel prepared for parent-teacher conferencing, you are not alone. Many veteran teachers avoid and are not comfortable in these situations. Experience is the best teacher. If a beginning teacher does not receive a background and a basic understanding of parent-teacher communication techniques, he or she may need to look for other sources of information on effective strategies. Learning on the job by acquiring information from colleagues can be helpful. Teachers can also search academic literature, where there is an extensive knowledge base.

Parents come to the table with their own agenda, and the teacher is usually there to react to their concerns. Occasionally, a teacher can react positively to their concerns about the student. Most of the time teachers are in a position that requires them to mitigate and litigate the student-teacher or student-curriculum-pedagogy relationship. Occasionally, the teacher is called to defend his or her practices. Here is a list of suggestions that can help:

• Collect phone numbers and addresses, and identify early which parent the students would like the teacher to communicate with. This includes work phone numbers. Put the information on file cards. This lets students and parents know the teacher is willing to be proactive in communicating with home. If a student's last name is different from the parent's, making sure the correct last name is used can be critically important in establishing rapport from the beginning of the conversation.

• Let parents know how they can best reach the teacher, through telephone calls, e-mail, or other strategies. Teachers can send the information home by mail or announce it during open house. The smart teacher will create a returnable parent acknowledgement of receiving the information and reward the student!

• If appropriate the teacher can make calls during school hours with the student present. After the teacher has spoken to the parents, parents often want to talk to their son or daughter. This works well with behavior problems. Students usually want to avoid these situations. Once a new teacher does this, the rest of the class will quickly get the message that parental relationships are important to the classroom teacher.

• Teachers should acknowledge potential trouble early and become proactive. The teacher can avoid getting calls by making calls home first. Often the call parents make won't be to the teacher; it will be to someone in the administration. A call at the first sign of trouble can often clear up misunderstandings early.

• It is important to realize that the classroom experience the student is taking home is filtered through the mind of that student. Teachers need to itemize and break down the potential issues ahead of time and prepare a response. Acknowledge the concerns the parents bring and prepare to redefine them from your perspective. It is helpful to remember that the teacher and the parents are on the same side, collaborators in the students' education.

• As a "new teacher on the block" try to talk to counselors, administrators, or other teachers familiar with the students or student before making calls or conferencing with parents. Sometimes even veteran teachers need help in dealing with certain parents. Teachers shouldn't put themselves in a position to be ambushed. If a teacher is really worried, it is perfectly fine to have a counselor or administrator familiar with the parents present and let the parents know they will be there.

• Sometimes it might be better for a teacher to let others familiar with the parents and students make the call. The teacher can then set up a conference if it is still necessary. A teacher shouldn't see this as a sign of weakness. It can be the best strategy. A vote of confidence directed toward the teacher by a trusted counselor or administrator can get around the school's community quickly and begin to build the new teacher's reputation as a caring and effective teacher and communicator. This can be a really necessary strategy for non-English-speaking parents!

- Once in a parent-teacher conference, the teacher should start the conference by listening carefully to what the parents have to say. Having itemized grades, lessons, handouts, student work, and so on will help. The teacher can then break down parent concerns and carefully address each one individually. Being organized and prepared with potential solutions to the problems a teacher expects to hear ahead of time can reap rewards in increased communication and rapport with parents.

- Letting supervisors know ahead of time about problems that could spill over into their laps allows teachers and supervisors to work on strategies together. Giving the supervisor copies of relevant materials (classroom policies, copies of tests, etc.) in advance so they are brought up to speed can help make the new teacher's job easier.

Precautions and Possible Pitfalls

Many times parent conferences turn out to be hugely successful. However, they can also turn sour. Occasionally parents simply will not be there for the teacher or their son or daughter. They may not have control over their relationship with their child themselves. Sad to say that phone calls home and parent conferences may be a lost cause in some cases. Counselors can often alert the teacher to situations where conferencing won't help. A teacher could end up listening to the parent's problems and never really resolve the issues with their student. In these cases, the teacher will need to follow through on the paperwork the school or district requires such as sending home notifications. However, sometimes teachers may need to accept the fact they are on their own and need to come up with strategies that won't include the parents.

Sources

Henderson, M. V., Hunt, S. N., & Day, R. (1993). Parent-teacher conferencing skills and pre-service programs. *Education, 114*(1), 71.

Rabbitt, C. (1984). The parent/teacher conference: trauma or teamwork. *Phi Delta Kappan, 59*, 471-472.

Strategy 90: Treat parents as part of the solution. Reach out to parents to form a partnership in educating elementary and high school students.

What the Research Says

Students want their parents to be involved in their education. A high level of parental involvement in children's education generally leads to a high level of academic achievement. Parents frequently are involved with their children's education while children are in elementary school, but often stop being involved once children are in high school. One study looked at 748 urban elementary and secondary school students' (Grade 5, $N = 257$; Grade 7, $N = 257$; Grade 9, $N = 144$; and Grade 11, $N = 90$) requests for and attitudes about their families' involvement in their education. Of these, 449 were black, 129 were Hispanic, and 121 were white. The study compared high- and low-achieving students in mathematics and English (or reading for elementary school students). It also examined whether there were ethnic differences in students' feelings about family involvement. Students in all grades requested parental assistance with schoolwork and had positive attitudes about using their parents as educational resources, although elementary students made more requests and had more positive attitudes than secondary school students. Both high- and low-achieving students showed interest in parental involvement. However, at the elementary school level, high-achieving Hispanic students in mathematics had more favorable attitudes than did lower-achieving Hispanic students in mathematics. Black and Hispanic students were generally more interested in parental involvement than were white students.

Classroom Applications

Teachers should reach out to parents to enhance their involvement and develop a partnership in their children's education. Many parents are unaware that they have the ability to have an impact on their children's education even if they are not well educated themselves. Teachers can explain and illustrate for parents how a parent can function as an educational manager or teacher. Some examples of the parent as manager are as follows:

1. Provide time, a quite place, and adequate light for studying. Help the child determine the best time and place to work.

2. Each night ask if there is a homework assignment and ask to see it when it has been completed.

3. Each night ask about what happened in school.

4. Have a dictionary accessible and encourage the child to use it.

5. Find out when tests are to be given and make sure the child has a good night's sleep and breakfast the day of the test.

6. Visit the school to discuss the child's progress and to find out what can be done at home.

7. Communicate positive attitudes and expectations about the child's school performance.

8. Avoid letting a child's household responsibilities assume more importance than schoolwork.

Prepare a handout for parents so they have some idea about what they can do at home to support this partnership.

Precautions and Possible Pitfalls

If parents do not speak English well, they may be reluctant to communicate with teachers. In such cases, if the teacher cannot speak the parent's language, a community volunteer might act as a school advocate and resource or someone from the school might be able to translate a letter or handout for parents into the parents' native language.

Sources

Hartman-Haas, H. J. (1983). *Family educational interaction: Focus on the child*. Paper presented at the annual meeting of the American Educational Research Association, Montreal, Canada.

Hartman-Haas, H. J. (1984). Family involvement tips for teachers. *Division of Research Evaluation and Testing Research Bulletin*, pp. 1-12. Newark, NJ: Newark Board of Education.

 Strategy 91: Make an extra effort to recruit minority and culturally diverse parents into the educational mix. They will make your classroom more culture-friendly.

What the Research Says

Each day America's schools face greater diversity than at any time since the turn of the 20th century. During the past two decades schools have taken in great numbers of students from Laos, Cambodia, Vietnam, and the Philippines. With families from Mexico, Central America, and the Caribbean, along with immigrants from China and Korea, all coming to the United States seeking more favorable job options, politically stable environments, and educational opportunities for their children, America's schools have never been more diverse. In Los Angeles Unified School District (the second largest in the United States), students speak some 80 different languages.

Studies of Latino immigrant families repeatedly show that the parents are highly interested in their children's education (Goldenberg & Gallimore, 1995). These parents, although they may be unfamiliar and uncomfortable with the American educational system, display a strong desire to see their children succeed and want to contribute to this success. Research with parents of minority and low-income students suggests they would like to be much more involved than they currently are in supporting their children's schools (Metropolitan Life, 1987). Studies including African American parents report the same high interest, but find that many of these parents lack the confidence that is necessary to support involvement (Chavkin & Williams, 1993).

Classroom Applications

The face of America's teacher is typically female, Caucasian, and monolingual. This reality poses some interesting challenges for involving parents of minority and culturally diverse parents in the education of their students.

The beginning teacher may feel somewhat apprehensive in recruiting parents of minority and culturally diverse students as resources in the classroom. This reluctance is based on a concern about language difficulties, possible cultural differences, or simply inexperience on the part of the new teacher. And yet, because of our changing population, the beginning teacher should expect a diverse population of students. The challenges now facing teachers in these diverse settings may require the need for social understanding that goes beyond the aspects of culture often approached in teacher education multicultural classes. Challenges include the proper handling of major holidays, religious customs, dress, and food. Even veteran teachers express a need for more intensive kinds of insight into the social ideals, values, and behavioral standards of each culture. They also require a more firm understanding of these standards and the cultural approaches to child rearing and schooling, first in the parent's own culture and then in the cultures these parents have passed down to their children.

Many new teachers focus on critical thinking and Socratic questioning techniques, which emphasize a student's active class participation (usually verbal). If students are from a cultural background that stresses quiet respect in school, they may need to be coaxed to become more active participants in their own learning. Teachers can speak with parents on why active participation is important to their child's education. Teachers can also provide alternative opportunities, such as allowing students to write journal entries or interact in small-group discussions.

Following are some suggestions new teachers can use to make their classrooms more culture-friendly and to promote students' values of helping and sharing:

- Select two classroom monitors representing two different cultures and encourage them to work together.
- Allow students to help each other study vocabulary (students with greater English proficiency help those with a lesser ability).
- Allow students to work in small groups to preview their homework assignments, discussing possible strategies for problems and ensuring that all understand the assignment. This also helps students whose parents may not be able to read the assignment in English.
- Use choral reading as well as individual reading.
- Have more than one "student of the week" so that the attention is shared.
- Share cleanup of the whole room at once, rather than having each group clean up an activity center before the children move to another (observed in a kindergarten classroom).
- Emphasize joint ownership of classroom crayons and other materials rather than doling out a box per child.

Precautions and Possible Pitfalls

Parents of culturally diverse students can be an untapped resource in today's classrooms. Care should be taken to keep parents informed through communication (either written or verbal) in the parent's native language, if their English is not proficient. Teachers must also be aware that just because they send home information in the parents' native language, the parents may still not be able to read or write in that language. It is not uncommon to find parents who have had no formal education. The more information teachers can have about their students, their family, and their cultural identity, the more teachers can best work with parents in supporting students' learning.

Sources

Goldenberg, C., & Gallimore, R. (1995). Immigrant Latino parents' values and beliefs about their children's education: Continuities and discontinuities across cultures and generations. In P. Pintrich & M. Maehr (Eds.), *Advances in achievement motivation* (Vol. 9, pp.183-228). Greenwich, CT: JAI Press.

Metropolitan Life. (1987). Study of minority parent involvement in schools. Cited in Chavkin, N. F., & Williams, D. L. (1993). Minority parents and the elementary school. In N. F. Chavkin (Ed.), *Families and schools in a pluralistic society* (pp.73-83). New York: State University of New York Press.

Trumbull, E., Greenfield, P. M., Rothstein-Fisch, C., & Quiroz, B. (2001). *Bridging cultures between home and school: A guide for teachers.* Mahwah, NJ: Lawrence Erlbaum.

Index

**CORWIN
PRESS**

The Corwin Press logo—a raven striding across an open book—represents the happy union of courage and learning. We are a professional-level publisher of books and journals for K-12 educators, and we are committed to creating and providing resources that embody these qualities. Corwin's motto is "Success for All Learners."